Projèt

Macroeconomics for
Developing Countries

Macroeconomics for Developing Countries

Paul Cook

Senior Lecturer in Economics,
University of Manchester

Colin Kirkpatrick

Professor of Development Economics,
University of Bradford

HARVESTER
WHEATSHEAF

New York   London   Toronto   Sydney   Tokyo   Singapore

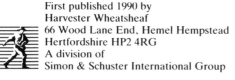

First published 1990 by
Harvester Wheatsheaf
66 Wood Lane End, Hemel Hempstead
Hertfordshire HP2 4RG
A division of
Simon & Schuster International Group

Typeset in 10/12pt Times
by Keyset Composition, Colchester

Printed and bound in Great Britain by
Billing and Sons Limited, Worcester

British Library Cataloguing in Publication Data

Cook, P. (Paul) 1944–
    Macroeconomics for developing countries: an introductory text.
    1. Developing countries. Macroeconomic policies.
    Formulation
    I. Title   II. Kirkpatrick, Colin 1944–
    339.091724

    ISBN 0-7450-0178-5
    ISBN 0-7450-0232-3 pbk

1 2 3 4 5   94 93 92 91 90

To Soyini, Khari, Susan and Stephen

Contents

Preface

This book has arisen out of the authors' experience in teaching introductory and intermediate level courses in macroeconomics to students studying the problems of Third World countries, many of whom are involved in economic policy formulation and implementation in their own countries on completion of their studies. Many others have been involved in work for international development agencies. In drawing up a course that would meet the needs of these students, two things became clear. The first was the absence of a suitable textbook. There are of course numerous excellent texts in development economics and in macroeconomics, but neither class of text exactly met our requirements. Economic growth, rather than short-run macro management, remains the dominant concern in development economics. Attention is concentrated on the contribution of aggregate supply to economic growth, in terms of either the productive use of unlimited supplies of labour, or the removal of particular supply constraints, such as a shortage of domestic savings or foreign exchange. On the other hand, in macroeconomic textbooks the analysis is conducted in terms of advanced, industrialised economies, with no attempt to adapt the framework to the particular conditions and characteristics of developing economies.

The second thing we quickly learnt from teaching the course was that students had considerable difficulty in relating the basic analytical models to current policy debates. There is a growing literature concerned with macro policy issues in less developed countries (LDCs), but much of this material is written at an advanced level in professional journals and is not easily assimilated by student readers, especially those who do not have a firm grounding in economic theory.

We have tried to overcome these two difficulties by showing how the standard textbook macroeconomic analysis can be adapted to incorporate particular features and conditions found in developing countries, and by then going on to use this framework to examine various macro policy issues of current concern to developing countries. Our attempt to provide a coverage of both theory and policy at an accessible level has inevitably involved simplification of what are complex and controversial issues. But on balance we believe that the potential dangers of over-simplification are out-weighed by the gains of encouraging students to bridge the gap between theory and practice at a comparatively early stage in their studies.

This book would not have been completed without the support and encouragement of colleagues and students. Peter Johns' persistent encouragement and tolerance of unmet deadlines con-tributed greatly to the completion of the book. Successive cohorts of students at Manchester and Bradford provided invaluable feedback on lecture presentations of the draft chapters. Barbara Evers helped at the final manuscript stage, and Jayne Hindle, Jean Hill and Anita Horne typed successive drafts with efficiency and good humour. Finally, we thank our families for having put up with our obsession with 'the book' and neglect of family duties over several years.

1

Introduction

The objective of macroeconomic policy is to control the short-run behaviour of an economy. The 'short run' is usually taken to cover a period of one to three years, and 'behaviour' is monitored by the movements in three main aggregate level variables – the output level, the inflation rate and the balance of payments. Short-run macroeconomic policy is often referred to as stabilisation policy. If we think of stability as a situation in which the main macro variables are at a desired or target level, then the need for stabilisation policy arises when the current rate of inflation, output level and balance of payments are not at these target levels. It is necessary, therefore, for the economy to 'adjust' from its current situation of instability to the target stabilised position.

Economic instability is reflected in high inflation, low output growth and a growing balance of payments deficit. The figures in Table 1.1 make it clear why short-run macroeconomic policy is critically important in developing countries. Each of the three main macro variables has fluctuated widely over the past decade. Growth in real output varied significantly from year to year. Inflation has been in excess of 25 per cent per annum throughout the decade. The goods and services account of the balance of payments has been in continuous deficit, with large annual fluctuations.

Table 1.1 Macro indicators for developing countries 1981–88

	1981	1982	1983	1984	1985	1986	1987	1988	1989
Inflation (annual % change)[1]	25.8	25.2	32.4	38.2	39.7	31.1	40.5	67.1	45.5
Current account balance (US$ billions)[2]	−68.0	−100.3	−82.7	−54.3	−51.2	−73.4	−32.1	−55.0	−57.0
Real GDP growth rate	1.9	2.2	2.2	4.1	3.6	4.2	3.3	4.3	3.3

[1]Consumer prices: weighted averages
[2]Goods and services balance

Source: International Monetary Fund (1989)

1.1 The national income accounting framework

We begin our analysis by reviewing what has become the focal point of macroeconomics, particularly the Keynesian variety, i.e. the aggregate income accounts. The macro level statistics are provided by the system of national accounts, and these accounting relationships can be used to provide important insights for the formulation of macro policy.

The central concept in national accounting is to measure the total output of goods and services of the economy over a given time period. This measure is known as gross domestic product (GDP). Output is produced by employing various factors of production (mainly labour and capital), and the revenue from the sale of output is used to make payments to these factors of production. The value of output is identical, therefore, to the value of incomes paid out, or what is known as national income. Since the output produced is sold (or added to stocks), the value of output is also equal to the value of expenditure. GDP can be regarded, therefore, as the total value of output produced (aggregate supply), the total value of expenditure on output (aggregate demand), or the total value of incomes generated in producing the output (real income).

The basic relations are a little more complicated when we allow for an economy's transactions with other countries. In an open economy, the total value of the output produced is purchased by either domestic or foreign residents. The part purchased by foreigners is exports. The part purchased by domestic residents is their total spending, less the amount spent on imports. The total spending of domestic residents is defined as absorption (A): if we deduct imports from absorption, then the remainder is spending on domestic output.

National income (Y) is given by total spending (domestic and foreign) on domestic goods, or

$$Y = A - M + X \qquad (1.1)$$
$$= A + (X - M) \qquad (1.2)$$

or,

$$(Y - A) = (X - M) \qquad (1.3)$$

($X - M$) is the difference between the values of exports and imports, and is known as the balance of trade. Relationship (1.3) tells us that the balance of trade is identically equal to the difference between national income (or the value of output, which is aggregate supply) and domestic absorption (which is aggregate demand).

Domestic residents may own factors of production abroad, and receive an income for their factor services rendered abroad. Similarly, the domestic economy may use factors whose owners reside abroad. These items (net factor payments, *NFP*) would need to be deducted from GDP to get a correct measure of final output produced by domestic residents. GDP plus *NFP* is called gross national product (GNP). If *NFP* is zero, then GDP and GNP are equal.

If *NFP* is zero, the trade balance $(X - M)$ is the same thing as the current account balance (CA). Thus, if there is a current account deficit (i.e. $M > X$), it is identically equal to the excess of spending by domestic residents over their income: aggregate demand exceeds aggregate supply.

Absorption was defined as total spending by domestic residents. Expenditure is made on consumption (C) and investment (I) goods (some of which may be imports). Expression (1.3) can therefore be rewritten as follows:

$$CA = X - M = Y - A = Y - (C + I) \tag{1.4}$$

The economy's balance of payments on current account is equal to the change (with opposite sign) in the stock of claims on the rest of the world (net acquisition of foreign assets, *NAFA*).

$$CA = X - M = \Delta NAFA \tag{1.5}$$

Savings is defined as the difference between income and consumption, i.e. $Y - C$. Therefore (1.4) can be rewritten as follows:

$$CA = X - M = Y - A = S - I \tag{1.6}$$

The current account deficit is identically equal to the level of net savings.

These national income identities can be used to illustrate the essence of the problem of macroeconomic stabilisation. If we assume that the private sector components of aggregate saving and investment are equal, so that net savings in the private sector are zero, then any difference between S and I must be due to an imbalance between public sector investment and savings. Thus, from (1.6), we can see that a balance of payments deficit on the current account will be matched by a budget deficit. This implies a fall in the country's stock of foreign assets, or an increase in the level of foreign liabilities. If this situation persists, a point will eventually be reached where the stock of foreign reserves is exhausted and/or no further foreign borrowing is possible. At this point, the economy must adjust, by lowering the level of domestic absorption relative to the level of output. In other words, the gap between aggregate supply and demand will have to be reduced.

1.2 Supply and demand imbalance

The previous section described the statistical framework within which macroeconomists work, and also introduced the notion that much of macroeconomic analysis is founded on the relation between aggregate demand and aggregate supply. We also saw that the need for stabilisation policy is generally signalled by excess demand pressures. It will be helpful at this stage to give a brief introduction to these important concepts, which underlie much of the macro analysis developed in the later chapters.

An aggregate supply curve shows the level of output that the total economy will supply at a given price level. If, for instance, in Figure 1.1, the price level is P_0, then suppliers are willing to produce Y_0 level of goods and services; if the price level is P_1 then Y_1 will in turn be produced. At this stage the price level has not been determined, only the decision to supply a certain amount at each different price level.

The reader will notice that the aggregate supply curve (AS) is drawn with an upward slope from left to right so that at higher price levels more output is provided. Obviously there will be a point when, given fixed amounts of capital, labour and technology, output cannot be increased in the short term. This represents the full employment level, and at this point the aggregate supply curve will become vertical.

Aggregate demand is the demand for goods and services as a whole, i.e. the demand for total output. The aggregate demand curve simply shows the relationship between the total amount of goods and services people desire and the price level. The curve constructed in Figure 1.1 and labelled AD is downward sloping

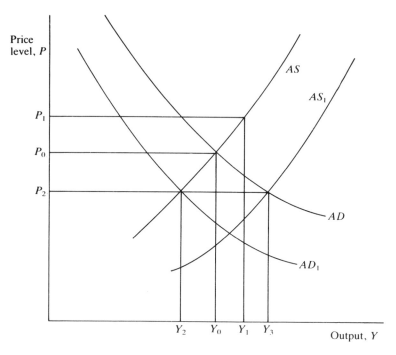

Figure 1.1 The effect of a reduction in aggregate demand and an increase in aggregate supply

from left to right, showing at each different price the level of output demanded.

The factors underlying these curves are quite complex and involve the decisions of individuals, businesses and government to both supply goods and services and demand them. In a real economy, decisions to supply will be affected by management objectives, which in turn will be affected by such things as the level of wages and the profits sought by people who own businesses. Demand is made largely by the same people who supply goods and services. Demand is affected in turn by the level of income and people's ability to pay. However, reflected in the aggregate demand curve is not simply the total demand for goods and services but also the demand for (and supply of) money. This is a more difficult concept that will be explained in the next two chapters. What needs to be understood at this stage is the fact that the two aggregate curves for supply and demand reflect the decisions to supply (produce) and demand (spend) of a wide range of individuals whose goals, tastes and preferences also differ widely.

The intersection of the *AS* and *AD* curves determines the equilibrium price and output levels. At the equilibrium price and output levels, P_0 and Y_0, economic agents on the demand and supply side of the economy are satisfied with what they are doing so there is no pressure for change. But suppose a disequilibrium exists, with the price level at P_2 and aggregate demand in excess of aggregate supply. How can the economy adjust to remove this disequilibrium?

A stabilisation policy will require the government to introduce economic measures that have the effect of lowering the level of aggregate demand, represented in Figure 1.1 by a leftwards shift in the *AD* curve to AD_1. Equilibrium is restored with price level P_2 and a lower output level Y_2. An alternative policy would be to shift the aggregate supply curve to the right; with equilibrium being restored at P_2 and Y_3. However, 'supply-side' policies typically take a long time to have an effect, so an immediate reduction in the economy's macro disequilibrium will have to rely mainly on 'demand-side' stabilisation policies.

The impact of a shift in the *AD* curve will depend on the shape of the *AS* curve. In Figure 1.2 we have drawn the *AS* curve in three sections – horizontal, upward sloping and vertical. What happens if *AD* increases? If *AS* is horizontal, output rises and the price level remains unchanged; if *AS* is vertical, the price level rises and output is unaltered; if *AS* is upward sloping, then both output and the price level increase. The shape of the *AS* curve is therefore critical in determining how a shift in aggregate demand will affect the price level.

Figure 1.3 illustrates the case of supply shifts. Provided the *AD* curve is downard sloping, then a shift in *AS* will always cause the price level and output level to move in opposite directions.

1.3 Economic structure and macroeconomic analysis

So far we have offered no explanation of the slope of the *AD* and *AS* curves. This will be the task of the following chapters. It is sufficient to note that the two curves represent the aggregation of all the separate markets within the economy. Each of these markets in turn

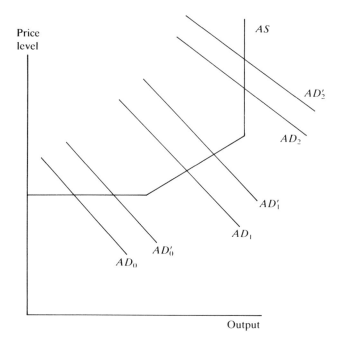

Figure 1.2 The effect of an increase in aggregate demand with different slopes for the aggregate supply curve

consists of individual consuming and producing agents. The shape of the *AD* and *AS* curves must therefore depend on the underlying market structure of the economy and the way in which economic agents behave within this structure. When we draw the aggregate demand and supply curves with a particular slope, or when we shift them in our analysis, we are implicitly assuming a certain underlying structure in the economy, and a given pattern of economic response by the economic agents within that structure. Economic policy issues cannot be discussed, therefore, without reference to particular economic structures and institutions, and economic models need to be formulated with structural characteristics appropriate to the economy at hand. The notion of a single model has to be replaced by a range of models, each of which is associated with a particular set of 'stylised facts' reflecting different structural and institutional conditions.

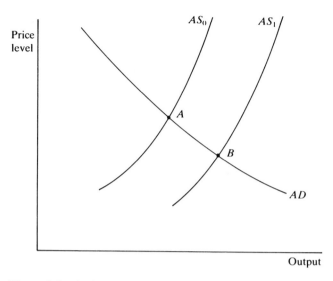

Figure 1.3 An increase in aggregate supply

There have been few attempts to allow for the important structural differences that exist between developed and developing economies. The type of economy discussed in macroeconomic textbooks is characterised by a large industrial sector, a well-trained, educated, wage-earning labour force, a developed financial system and a fully integrated structure of markets. In contrast, the typical features of the developing economy include poorly integrated markets, a large rural sector and widespread under-utilisation of labour. The type of economic structure and institutional framework we assume in our model of the economy will determine the results we obtain from our analysis. What we want to avoid, therefore, is the uncritical application of advanced economy models to the very different conditions found in the developing countries.

There is an obvious tension between the argument that each country has to be studied in the light of its own conditions, and the attempt to provide a general analytical framework for the study of macroeconomic policy in developing countries in general. There are, of course, important structural differences between developing countries themselves, in the level of per capita income, stage of industrialisation, dependence on trade, and so on. The way in which we try to resolve this problem is to identify certain 'stylised facts', as to the structural features of a 'typical' developing country. Few countries will display all of these characteristics, but most are likely to have some of them. By showing how these characteristics affect the macroeconomic stabilisation process, it should be possible for students to apply a similar analysis using the particular combination of features that best describes the economy in which they are interested.

1.4 Plan of the book

In the next four chapters we set out the basic macroeconomic model framework. We begin with aggregate demand and supply in the closed economy and the determination of the equilibrium output and price levels. We then give a more detailed discussion of the monetary sector and the determination of the money supply. We complete the basic model by introducing the open economy dimension. The next step is to provide a link between theory and policy, by discussing the role of policy instruments and targets. The remainder of the book is devoted to the discussion of policy issues, with separate chapters that discuss fiscal and monetary policy, balance of payments policy and inflation policy. The final chapter examines stabilisation policy, and includes a discussion of the impact of both demand- and supply-side policies in the developing economy context.

Further reading

Artis (1984) gives a clear explanation of the national income accounting framework. Khan (1987) provides a general overview of macroeconomic adjustment policy in developing countries, and Khan and Knight (1982) discuss the distinction between demand- and supply-side policies for correcting macro disequilibrium. The arguments concerning structural differences and appropriate model frameworks are given in Taylor (1983). The student is also encouraged to consult recent issues of the World Bank's *World Development Report* and the various statistical publications of the International Monetary Fund.

2

Aggregate demand in the closed economy

The aim of this and the following two chapters is to set out a simple model of macroeconomic behaviour based on the standard expenditure analysis. At this stage, no attempt is made to take account of the structural differences that exist between developed and less developed countries; nor do we try to relate the analysis explicitly to the macro stabilisation problems of developing countries. This will be the task of subsequent chapters.

Simplifying assumptions are needed if we are to develop a framework that portrays the macroeconomic workings of an economy. We begin by making four such assumptions. First, it will be assumed that the economy's output level is entirely demand determined, i.e. businesses, firms or enterprises are able to supply all that is demanded. In terms of Figure 1.2 in the previous chapter, this means that the aggregate supply curve is horizontal. Second, the assumption of a perfectly elastic supply curve in turn allows us to assume that prices are fixed and are determined exogenously, outside the analytical framework. Third, we assume that the economy is a closed one, with no transactions with the rest of the world. Finally, it is assumed that there is no government sector. Each of these assumptions will be removed as the analysis progresses.

2.1   Aggregate demand and the goods market

The equilibrium condition is that aggregate demand and supply should be equal. Since aggregate supply has been assumed to respond to the level of aggregate demand, we focus attention on the determination of the level of demand. At this stage, supply can be described as acting passively, although in subsequent chapters this restrictive assumption will be dropped since the behaviour of the supply side of the economy becomes an important component of a macroeconomic framework for developing countries.

Total desired expenditure, or aggregate demand, can be divided into expenditure for consumption and investment purposes. Since we have assumed a closed economy with no government sector, we can think of aggregate expenditure (E) as comprising private domestic expenditure by individuals or households on consumption (C) and by enterprises on investment (I). Broadly, consumption can be thought of as expenditure on goods and services that satisfy an immediate want, while investment contributes to satisfying the wants of society in the future by increasing an economy's potential for supplying consumption goods. Thus,

$$E = C + I \qquad (2.1)$$

At this stage, we will not consider in any detail what determines the level of consumption and investment demand. We simply assume that households' consumption is for the most part determined by their personal disposable income. More specifically, we assume that consumption is a linear function of income. As income rises, consumption rises, but by less than the rise in income. The consumption function therefore takes the following form:

$$C = a + bY \qquad (2.2)$$

which says that consumption is equal to an autonomous component, a, which is unrelated to income, and to income through bY, where b is the marginal propensity to consume and is given by the slope of the consumption function.

We will initially assume that investment expenditure is also autonomous. The aggregate expenditure function is therefore the sum of consumption and investment, as shown in Figure 2.1 by $C + I$.

The equilibrium output level is determined where aggregate

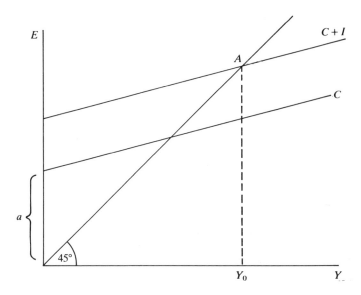

Figure 2.1   The aggregate expenditure function for consumption and investment

demand, or planned aggregate expenditure, is equal to aggregate supply, the output that is actually produced. This is shown in Figure 2.1 by the 45° line which joins all points at which aggregate demand is equal to output. Expenditure for consumption and investment is measured on the vertical axis, and the quantity of goods and services produced (real income) is measured on the horizontal axis. Point A is the only point on the aggregate demand schedule which is also on the 45° line. The level of output corresponding to this point, Y_0, is therefore the equilibrium level of output (or real income). We assume that, in disequilibrium situations, supply responds to changes in demand. Therefore, if output is below the equilibrium level, there is excess demand and output rises. If output is greater than demand, there will be excess supply and output contracts.

The condition for equilibrium can be expressed in another way. Equilibrium occurs where aggregate expenditure ($E = C + I$) is equal to aggregate output, or income. The income received by households that is not spent on consumption is saved.

$$Y = C + S \qquad\qquad (2.3)$$

Therefore, since in equilibrium $E = Y$, then

$$C + I = C + S \qquad (2.4)$$

or

$$I = S$$

This means that, since the income not used for consumption purposes by households is saved and since the only other form of expenditure identified besides consumption is investment, then this surplus is used for investment.

2.2   Simple multiplier

Even with the simple demand-oriented framework developed so far the interrelationship between demand (aggregate expenditure) and real output (aggregate supply) is quite complex. The working of the simple framework outlined in Figure 2.1 above can be illustrated by changing one of the components of expenditure, either consumption or investment. Assume desired investment rises from I to I_1, which in turn shifts $C + I$ to $C + I_1$ as shown in Figure 2.2. Initially equilibrium was obtained at A where $Y_0 = C + I$, which can be expressed in the functional form

$$Y_0 = a + bY_0 + I \qquad (2.5)$$

If desired or planned investment rises from I to I_1 (shown by the change in investment ΔI), then our equation becomes

$$Y_0 < \Delta I + a + bY_0 + I \qquad (2.6)$$

It can be seen that desired expenditure is no longer in equilibrium with real income. Desired expenditure now exceeds real income by the change in investment. Since we have assumed that our economy is demand driven, output or real income will adjust to changes in demand whenever they occur. Equation (2.6) can be amended to reflect the response of output to a change in demand (investment).

$$Y_0 + \Delta I < b\Delta I + \Delta I + a + bY_0 + I \qquad (2.7)$$

It can be seen in equation (2.7) that the system is still in disequilibrium because, although output changed in response to the initial change in demand (ΔI), this in turn was followed by another

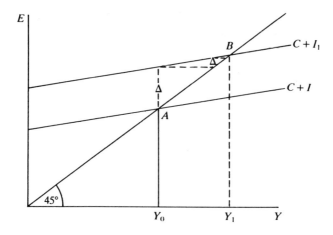

Figure 2.2 The effect of a rise in investment

change in demand ($b\Delta I$). This occurs because the relationship specified is two-way. Real income or output will always change in response to a change in aggregate demand, but aggregate demand itself changes whenever real income changes. This can clearly be seen in the formulation of the consumption function which specifies that consumption (a component of aggregate demand) is related to income so that it changes whenever income is changed.

To recap, an initial change in demand will bring about a change in income, which in turn will induce further changes in demand. What then prevents this process from continuing *ad infinitum*? You will notice from Figure 2.2 that the process comes to a halt when Y_1 is reached at the new equilibrium point *B*. If the dotted arrows are followed between points *A* and *B*, it can be observed that the changes in expenditure induced by each change in income after the initial change in investment become successively smaller. They in fact can be represented by a geometric progression. The total change between Y_0 and Y_1 becomes

$$\Delta Y = \Delta I + b\Delta I + b^2\Delta I + b^3\Delta I + b^4\Delta I \ldots \quad (2.8)$$

and if it is assumed that the change in aggregate expenditure in response to a change in income is less than the change in income (i.e. $b < 1$), then the process can be condensed to

$$\Delta Y = \Delta I(1 + b + b^2 + b^3 + b^4 \ldots) \quad (2.9)$$

so that the effect of a change in investment on income is given by

$$\Delta Y = \Delta I \frac{1}{1-b} \tag{2.10}$$

This last term is known as the investment multiplier, which shows the size of the effect that a change in investment has on income. Crucial to the size of this effect is the value assigned to b. The higher the value of b, the larger the effect on income through the multiplier process. The concept of the multiplier is taken up again in the appendix to this chapter in the context of the *IS/LM* framework, and later in Chapter 7 where it is discussed in relation to changes in the rate of interest and price level.

Up until now we have treated the level of investment as autonomous. Let us consider what factors are likely to influence the investment decision. In an economy with no government sector, investment is undertaken using resources that are either borrowed or generated internally by firms. In either case we assume that the rate of interest will strongly influence the decision to undertake investment. In the case of a firm borrowing funds for investment, the rate of interest represents the price paid for the funds. At any given time, there will be a number of possible investment projects, each of which has a different expected rate of return. At high rates of interest, it can be expected that only the most profitable projects will be undertaken, and as the interest rate falls projects with lower expected returns can be undertaken. The rate of interest is also important for the firm that is considering whether to use its own internal funds for financing investment. In this case the firm will again compare the return from the project with the rate of interest it would earn by lending the funds to someone else. We might expect, therefore, to find an inverse relationship between the rate of interest (r) and the level of investment, as shown in Figure 2.3.

2.3   Equilibrium in the goods market

So far we have been discussing the determination of the flow of real goods and services in the economy. A number of simple assumptions have been made concerning the determinants of consumption and investment. Relationships between consumption and income,

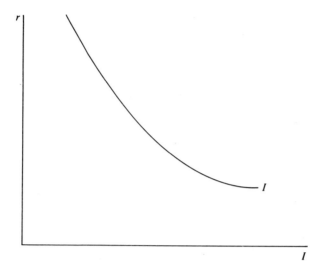

Figure 2.3   The investment function

and investment and the rate of interest, were considered. Without refining our analysis of the behaviour underlying these relationships at this stage, they can now be combined by use of a four quadrant diagram, Figure 2.4. The consumption relationship is produced in the SE quadrant in the form of a savings function. Instead of showing the linear relation between consumption and income, we have plotted its inverse, the relationship between savings (that part of income not consumed) and income. In that case, the lower vertical axis measures the level of saving. In the NW quadrant the investment function is shown, with the level of investment varying inversely with the interest rate (note that this diagram is the same as the one used in Figure 2.3 except that the level of investment is recorded from right to left instead of left to right). In the SW quadrant a 45° line is drawn, which permits the investment level to be equated to savings. These three quadrants can now be used to fill the fourth. The student will observe that we have used familiar diagrams back to front and in some cases have used the inverse of relationships previously described. This is common in economics and the student should quickly get used to the practice.

The procedure can easily be followed by beginning at some point

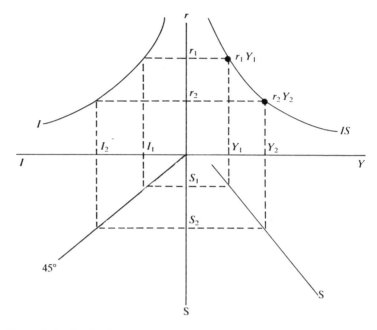

Figure 2.4   Derivation of the *IS* curve representing saving and investment
behaviour

on the investment axis, say I_1. From the investment function we can
see that this is consistent with a particular rate of interest r_1. Now
drop down to the 45° line and across to S_1 on the savings axis; then
into the savings function quadrant; and then up into the NE
quadrant. When that line reaches the interest rate level r_1, it has
established a point at which the goods market is in equilibrium at a
particular combination of income and interest rate. In other words,
at the point indicated by $r_1 Y_1$ the level of investment given by
the rate of interest r_1 is equal to the rate of saving S_1 given by the
level of income Y_1.

The same procedure is then repeated for various points on the
investment function. Trace the point starting with the interest rate
level r_2 and end up with $r_2 Y_2$. If we join up the various equilibrium
points in the NE quadrant, we obtain the *IS* curve (the investment
savings curve), which defines equilibrium in the goods market at
different combinations of interest rate and income.

2.4 The money market

In the preceding section we discussed aggregate demand and the goods market, where we were interested in the flows of output of real goods and services in the economy. In this section we introduce a new market, the market for financial assets. An asset is a means of holding wealth, and is held by individuals for the return that it yields. There are many kinds of asset traded in markets, but we shall for the present time assume that only financial assets exist.

At any given time, individuals have to decide how to allocate their total wealth between different financial assets. This is known as a portfolio decision. To simplify the analysis, we will limit the discussion to two types of financial asset – money and bonds. Our definition of money includes notes and coins and cheque book facilities. Money represents a convenient way of holding financial wealth since it can be used for immediate transactions. On the other hand, it has the disadvantage of not yielding a financial return. Bonds, the other type of financial asset, are paper securities which promise to pay the holder a certain amount of money at specified times in the future. To illustrate in a simple manner the working of a financial market we consider here a type of bond which pays a fixed amount to the holder for as long as the bond is held.

The market price of the bond will then depend on this fixed amount and the market rate of interest. Suppose the bond is to pay £4 each year and the market rate of interest is 4 per cent: the market price of the bond will then be £100, since the rate of return it yields is equal to the market interest rate. If the market rate of interest falls to 3 per cent, the market price will rise to £133.3, to equate the return on the bond (£4 as a rate of return on £133.3) to the market interest rate. We can see, therefore, that this is an inverse relationship between the bond price and its yield or interest rate.

Let us recap on where we have got to so far. If the level of financial wealth is fixed – in other words, if there is a wealth budget constraint – and if there are only two financial assets, then individuals through portfolio decisions allocate their wealth between the two assets. The decision on how much money to hold also determines how much wealth is held in the form of the other asset, bonds, so we can discuss the financial assets market by concentrating only on the money market. As in every other market, equilibrium will be determined by the supply and demand relations. We therefore next consider the demand and supply of money.

2.5 Demand for money

Three motives are commonly identified for the demand for money, whether by households or enterprises. The transactions demand arises from individuals' need for money to meet their day-to-day spending requirements. The amount they decide to hold for these purposes will depend mainly on the level of income: the higher the level of income, the greater the volume of transactions and hence the greater the transactions demand for money. The second factor is the precautionary motive, by which we refer to money held to meet imperfectly foreseen contingencies. This demand is also likely to vary positively with the level of income.

A third element in the demand for money is identified as the speculative motive. Holding financial wealth in the alternative form to money, i.e. bonds, means there is the risk of incurring a capital loss (or making a gain) if the actual rate of interest diverges from the rate the purchasers of the bond expect when making their purchase. The speculator who is willing to make a guess about the future price of bonds will move into and out of bonds since it is likely that capital gains and losses can be made from trading bonds. If the purchaser expects bond prices to fall in the future, he or she will hold money until the price actually falls, and will then buy into bonds. Now recall that the price of bonds varies inversely with the market rate of interest. The rate of interest can therefore be taken as a proxy for speculators' expectations of capital gains and losses on bonds. If interest rates are low, the expectation will be for a rise in interest rates, and a fall in bond prices, so speculators will demand money (or, more formally, money balances). The opposite occurs when interest rates are high. Therefore, we expect to find an inverse relationship between the rate of interest and the speculative demand for money.

The total demand for money, a combination of the above three motives for holding money, is therefore a positive function of the level of income, and a negative function of the rate of interest. The relationship is shown in Figure 2.5. The interest rate (r) is shown on the vertical axis and the amount of money demanded on the horizontal axis. Each demand curve for money represents a specific income level such that $Y_3 > Y_2 > Y_1$.

In practice, at lower levels of income the demand for money curve is likely to slope steeply upward towards the left-hand side.

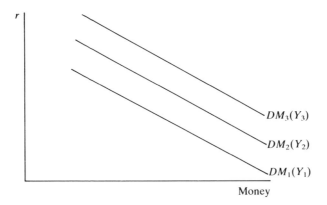

Figure 2.5   The demand for money function

This is because at low levels of income the demand for money for transactions purposes will dominate an individual's demand for money, and for essential purchases will be insensitive to the rate of interest. In this case the curve will have an upward-sloping tail parallel to the rate of interest axis.

2.6   Equilibrium in the money market

To determine the equilibrium in the money market we need to introduce the supply of money. The supply of money is controlled by the government through the Central Bank (in Chapter 3 we consider in detail how the Central Bank exercises this control), and for the moment we assume that the supply of money is given. This is shown by the vertical *SM* line in Figure 2.6.

A higher level of income is associated with a higher demand for money schedule, shown in Figure 2.6 by the curves $DM_1(Y_1)$, $DM_2(Y_2)$, etc. Figure 2.6 also shows that an upward shift in the demand for money schedule will lead to an increase in the rate of interest if the supply of money remains unchanged. Suppose that the rate of interest is r_1 and the demand for money schedule is increased from $DM_1(Y_1)$ to $DM_2(Y_2)$. In this situation the demand for money is greater than the supply of money, the excess being shown by the dotted line. Given that only two financial assets exist,

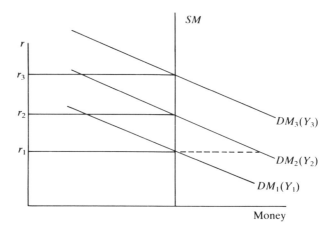

Figure 2.6   Demand and supply of money with different income levels

money and bonds, economic agents will attempt to increase their money balances by selling bonds. These will be sold at a price below which they were priced before the increase in the demand for money took place. As there is an inverse relationship between the price of the bonds and the interest rate, interest rates will rise to r_2. At this point everyone is satisfied with their respective holdings of money and bonds. It is important to point out at this stage that the total money supply has remained unchanged. Individuals attempt to get more money by trading their financial assets with others in the economy. The interest rate acts as a rationing mechanism since everyone cannot obtain more money without a change in the total money supply.

Figure 2.7 gives an alternative representation of how equilibrium in the money market is reached. The NW quadrant shows that the speculative demand for money falls as the interest rate rises. The curve is drawn as convex to the origin because at very low interest rates individuals will become increasingly certain of a future increase in the rate, and will therefore hold a high proportion of their portfolio in money. The opposite situation occurs when the interest rate is very high, so the speculative demand curve is almost vertical.

The transactions and precautionary demands – shown in the SE

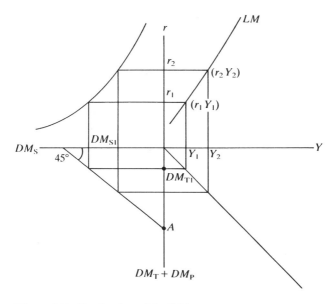

Figure 2.7 Derivation of the *LM* curve

quadrant – are a positive function of the level of income. The SW quadrant represents the fixed supply of money: the greater the level of money supply, the further out from the origin the 45° line will lie. The 45° line is drawn from the speculative demand axis to the transactions demand axis to show that the total demand for money adds up to the total money supply. If, for example, speculative demand is zero, the transactions and precautionary demands will equal the money supply (point *A*). Any point on the line gives a combination of the two components that adds up to the total.

We can now fill in the remaining NE quadrant. Begin in the NW quadrant with the demand for money for speculative purposes DM_{S1} and interest rate r_1: using the SW quadrant allows us to derive the transaction demand DM_{T1}; up to income Y_1; giving a point r_1Y_1 in the NE quadrant. We can repeat this process for another interest rate r_2, producing point r_2Y_2. If we join up the points in the NE quadrant, we get an upward sloping *LM* curve, showing combinations of income and interest rate at which the money market (i.e. the supply of and demand for money) is in equilibrium.

2.7   Equilibrium in the goods and money markets

We have now studied the conditions that must be satisfied if the goods and money markets are to be in equilibrium. But neither market on its own can solve the equilibrium level of income and interest rate, since in each case we have one equation with two unknowns. Notice, however, that both markets show equilibrium conditions for the same unknowns, i.e. income and interest rate, so if we combine our two markets we have two equations in two unknowns, and we can solve simultaneously the equilibrium values of the rate of interest and income. This is shown as Y_0 and r_0 in Figure 2.8.

We have now obtained an equilibrium point E_0 at which both the goods market and the money market are in equilibrium. The equilibrium point will alter if either the *IS* or *LM* curve shifts. Suppose the *IS* curve shifts to the right from IS_0 to IS_1. This could be the result of an autonomous rise in consumption expenditure (check back to Figure 2.4 to make sure you understand this point). The increase in demand causes output to rise, but the rise in income increases the transaction demand for money. With the supply of money fixed, the interest rate has to rise in order to reduce speculative demand, keeping the total demand and supply of money equal. The increase in the rate of interest, however, will lead to a reduction in investment demand. Thus, the increase in income in Figure 2.8 (Y_0Y_1) is less than the horizontal shift in the *IS* curve. The *LM* curve does not shift because the supply of money is unchanged. The change in the interest rate is seen as a movement along the *LM* curve.

Suppose that the *LM* curve shifts to the right as a result of an increase in the supply of money (Figure 2.9). The increase in the quantity of money causes the interest rate to fall in order to maintain equilibrium in the money market by increasing speculative demand. The fall in interest rates causes investment to increase and hence income to rise, leading to a rise in transactions demand for money. Hence the overall reduction in the interest rate (r_0r_1) is less than the initial (vertical) shift in the *LM* curve. The shift in the *LM* curve leads to a movement along the *IS* curve. In this and in the previous example, the initial disequilibrium occurs in only one of the markets. In both cases, the other market responds to the initial disequilibrium (represented by shifts in the respective curves) but is

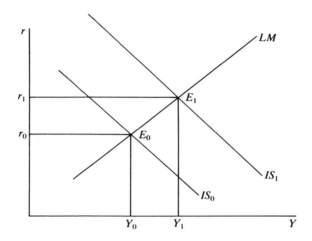

Figure 2.8 The effect of a shift in the *IS* curve holding the *LM* curve constant

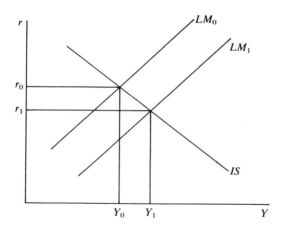

Figure 2.9 The effect of a shift in the *LM* curve holding the *IS* curve constant

not itself in disequilibrium (seen by movements along the equilibrium curve).

Later chapters will consider in much greater detail the different shapes the *IS* and *LM* curves may take, and the ways in which the economy may respond to shifts in the curves. A more formal algebraic presentation of the *IS/LM* framework is given in the appendix to this chapter.

2.8   Government in the closed economy

We now extend the basic model to include the government sector. The government has a direct means of influencing the behaviour of the economy by varying the level of government expenditure and taxation. This is known as fiscal policy. Government expenditure (*G*) is itself a component of aggregate demand, and changing taxes will affect the expenditure of individuals, households and enterprises.

For the moment we will assume that the level of government expenditure is policy determined and does not depend upon the workings of the model. With government expenditures exogenously determined, these can be graphically represented by moving the *IS* curve parallel to the right. In Figure 2.4 the investment curve in the NW quadrant shifts further out from the origin as government investment expenditure is added to the schedule. In the SE quadrant the savings function now cuts the *Y* axis further to the right. Consideration of Figure 2.1 shows why: government recurrent expenditure shifts the *C* curve upwards, increasing the size of *a*. The level of income associated with zero savings ($Y = C$) is therefore increased. The result of the shift in the investment schedule and the savings schedule is to move the *IS* curve to the right in Figure 2.4.

Incorporating government revenue from taxation into the model requires some modification of the behavioural relationships between desired expenditure and income. Direct tax payments reduce the level of income out of which consumption is made. On the other hand, households receive certain transfers from the government which increase the households' income. If we treat transfer payments as negative taxation, we can treat taxation as the 'net' amount paid by the households. Indirect taxation is more difficult to handle in our framework since it is levied entirely on expenditure and therefore reduces disposable income indirectly, by raising the price of goods and services purchased from income.

The simplest way of including taxation in the model is to assume a linear relation between tax revenue and the level of income:

$$T = t_0 + t_1 Y \tag{2.11}$$

where T is total tax receipts, t_0 is taxes unrelated to income, and t_1 is income-related taxes. Substituting into the consumption function gives

$$
\begin{aligned}
C &= a + b(Y - T) \\
&= a + bY - bT \\
&= a + bY - bt_0 - bt_1 Y
\end{aligned} \tag{2.12}
$$

2.9 Fiscal policy

Fiscal policy consists of changes in taxation and government spending, i.e. changes in G, t_0 and t_1. We can now incorporate these policy variables into our basic model. We have seen already how an increase in aggregate expenditure and therefore government expenditure will move the IS curve to the right. From Figure 2.8 we can see that an increase in government expenditure, shown by the shift in the IS curve from IS_0 to IS_1, results in an increase in income and the rate of interest. The increase in government expenditure causes excess demand at the original interest rate, and as income increases, the demand for money also rises, causing the interest rate to begin to increase. This process continues until a new equilibrium is reached at $Y_1 r_1$.

The impact of a change in government taxation can be analysed in a similar fashion to expenditure. A reduction in taxes shifts the IS curve in the same direction to an increase in government expenditure. There is one important difference to note, however. The impact of a given change in taxation on income will not be the same as the impact of the same amount of government expenditure. The reason is straightforward. Taxation is paid from income and represents a 'cost' in terms of consumption and savings forgone. If taxes are reduced, therefore, only a fraction (b) of the increase in income will be used for increased consumption expenditure. Hence the impact on income of a tax change will be less than an equivalent amount of increased government expenditure. The impact of changes in government expenditure and taxation is examined in greater detail in Chapter 7.

2.10   Aggregate demand and the price level

We can begin to consider the role of prices in the analysis by examining the implications of a discrete increase in the price level (this is not the same thing as inflation, which involves a continuous increase in the price level). We will assume that the price level is given to the model exogenously, affecting the system but not in turn affected by it. We cannot discuss the determination of the price level until we have completed an analysis of the supply side of the economy.

It is important that the student understands how the variables developed so far in our framework are specified. The framework incorporates four major elements – consumption, investment, the demand for money and the supply of money. We must consider whether these are specified in real or money terms (sometimes referred to as nominal terms). Will changes in the price level affect these relationships? If the answer is no, then they are formulated in real terms. With regard to consumption and investment expenditure, these can be considered to be specified in real terms rather than in nominal or money terms. Changes in prices will not affect or alter their behavioural relationships. For example, if prices rise, then consumption decisions remain the same because both the demand for goods and services, and levels of income (which determine consumption) rise equally. Similarly, decisions about investment are unaffected by price changes because even though the cost of investment rises as prices rise, so do the expected benefits accruing from investment. This means that the *IS* curve is unaffected by changes in the price level. This situation will be changed in Chapter 5 when international trade is introduced.

In our discussion of the money market we discussed the various motives for holding money balances. We must now be more precise and distinguish between the nominal and real value of money balances. The nominal value or quantity of money does not change with a change in the price level. But an increase in the price level does reduce the real value of money since the purchasing power of money will decline.

It is evident from our discussion of the motives for demanding money balances that they are held mainly in order to obtain real goods and services. The demand for money curves constructed can therefore be considered as a demand for real cash balances. Whenever the price level increases, the demand for money is assumed to increase in line with the level of income. The supply of money curve, however, was expressed in nominal or money terms. An increase in the price level will reduce the real value of the money supply, and the money supply curve in Figure 2.6 has to be thought of as being constructed on the basis of a specific price level. We therefore need to draw a series of money supply curves for different price levels, where the nominal supply of money is the same in each case, but the real money supply alters with the price level.

We are now in a position to see the effect of a change in the price level on the level of aggregate demand. For a given nominal money supply, higher price levels will be shown by the LM curve moving to the left, as in Figure 2.10, where $P_2 > P_1 > P_0$. These curves represent different levels of real money supply.

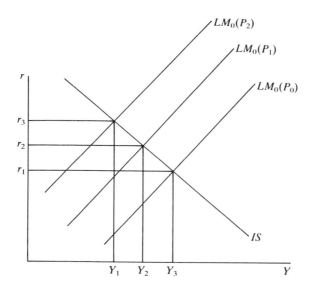

Figure 2.10 The effect of different price levels on the LM curve

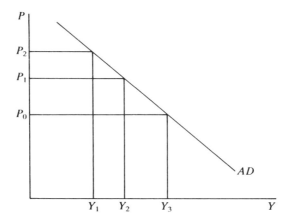

Figure 2.11 Derivation of the aggregate demand curve

The demand for money function and the functions underlying the *IS* curve are constructed independently of the price level, i.e. in real terms. From Figure 2.10 we can see that there is a unique, equilibrium level of real income associated with each price level. When the price level is high, at P_2, the corresponding level of income is low, at Y_1; lower price levels are associated with higher levels of real income.

The price levels associated with each real income level can be plotted as in Figure 2.11, to give the aggregate demand curve. The *AD* curve is downward sloping, showing that aggregate demand will increase if the price level falls. This is the case because when prices fall, the *LM* shifts to the right and interest rates fall. However, interest rates stimulate investment, so aggregate demand and income increase.

So far we have assumed that an increase in demand is matched by an increase in output: in other words, that supply is demand determined. In the next chapter we examine in more detail how supply responds to demand by considering what determines supply.

Further reading

Useful texts which extend the analysis in a similar framework are Parkin and Bade (1982, in particular ch. 20–2), Perlman (1974),

Cobham (1987) and Bronfenbrenner (1979). For a discussion of consumption and savings behaviour in developing countries the reader is referred to a series of articles by Houthakker (1961, 1965), Williamson (1968), Mikesell and Zinser (1973) and Lahini (1989). The determinants and characteristics of investment are covered in Blejer and Khan (1984) and Tun Wai and Wong (1982). For the money side of the economy see particularly Fry (1988).

Appendix: Derivation of the *IS* and *LM* curves

The simple *IS/LM* framework covers two sectors, the goods sector and the money sector. The variables are specified in real terms. At this stage, the model is a demand-oriented one since changes on the supply side are determined by events taking place on the demand side. Total supply or real income simply acts passively. The simple model does not incorporate the price level.

The model has a number of endogenous variables, the value of these variables being found in the solution of the equation system. These are savings, investment, the demand for money, real income and the rate of interest. On the other hand, a number of exogenous variables are also required. Such variables are provided from outside the equation system and must, therefore, be specified prior to the solution of the system. The model is specified in the following way:

Savings	$S = -a + (1 - b)Y$	(1)
Investment	$I = g_0 - g_1 r$	(2)
	$S = I$	(3)
Demand for money	$DM = j_1(Y) + u - j_2 r$	(4)
Supply of money	$SM = M_0$	(5)
	$SM = DM$	(6)

In this system:

a represents the amount of consumption not related to changes in income.

$(1 - b)$ represents the marginal propensity to save.

$(1 - b) < 1$ but > 0.

g_0 represents the amount of investment that is undertaken irrespective of movements in the rate of interest.

g_1 is the ratio of change in investment to a change in interest rates, where g_1 is < 0.

j_1 is the ratio of change in the transactions balances (MT) to a change in the level of income, where $j_1 > 0$.

j_2 is the ratio of the change in speculative balances (MS) to a change in the rate of interest, where $j_2 < 0$.

Total demand for money is obtained by summing the two equations

$$MT = j_1(Y)$$
$$MS = u - j_2 r$$
$$DM = MT + MS$$

The system can be solved by substituting the savings function and the investment function into the equality equation $S = I$. This gives

$$-a + (1 - b)Y = g_0 - g_1 r$$

and solving for r in terms of Y gives the equation for the IS curve

$$r = \frac{g_0 + a}{g_1} - \frac{(1 - b)}{g_1}(Y)$$

The first component on the right-hand side of the equation $g_0 + a/g_1$ represents the intercept of the IS curve with the vertical axis.

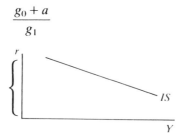

$$\frac{g_0 + a}{g_1}$$

If we increase $g_0 + a/g_1$ it will raise the intercept and shift the complete IS curve to the right. The second component $- (1 - b)/g_1$ represents the slope of the IS curve, the negative sign in front indicating that the curve slopes downwards to the right. In essence the larger the term $(1 - b)$, the marginal propensity to save, the steeper the slope of the *IS* curve. The larger the term g_1, the less steep the function.

The money sector can be dealt with in a similar manner. Substituting the equations *SM* and *DM* into the equality *SM* = *DM* we get

$$j_1(Y) + u - j_2 r = M_0$$

Solving for *r* again in terms of *Y* we produce

$$r = \frac{u - M_0}{j_2} + \frac{j_1}{j_2}(Y)$$

This represents the equation for the *LM* curve. The term $u - M_0/j_2$ represents the intercept of the curve with the vertical axis.

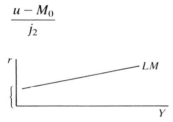

Similarly, an increase in this intercept term will shift the *LM* curve to the left. The ratio term j_1/j_2 shows the slope of the *LM* curve, and has a positive sign to indicate that it slopes upwards to the right. Thus the higher is the level of income (*Y*), the higher is the rate of interest (*r*) at which *DM* and *SM* are brought into equality.

The equilibrium condition can be found by integrating the *IS* and *LM* curves. Solving for each curve alone will not reveal the level of income (*Y*) which gives the equilibrium situation in the money and the goods sectors. To find the equilibrium level of *Y* (the point where the *LM* and *IS* curves intersect) we must eliminate the term *r* from the equations for both the *IS* and *LM* curves. This can be accomplished by setting the right-hand side of the equation for the *IS* curve and the *LM* curve equal to one another:

$$\frac{g_0 + a}{g_1} - \frac{(1 - b)}{g_1}(Y) = \frac{u - M_0}{j_2} + \frac{j_1}{j_2}(Y)$$

Rearranging terms to give the two terms in Y on the left and factoring out Y will give

$$Y\left(\frac{(1-b)}{g_1} + \frac{j_1}{j_2}\right) = \frac{g_0 + a}{g_1} - \frac{u - M_0}{j_2}$$

and

$$Y = \frac{1}{\dfrac{1-b}{g_1} + \dfrac{j_1}{j_2}}\left[\frac{g_0 + a}{g_1} - \frac{u - M_0}{j_2}\right]$$

Finally we can go on to find out what the effect of changing any of the exogenous components is on the equilibrium values of Y and r (and consequently how consumption, investment and monetary demand change).

If we multiply the numerator and the denominator through by g_1 we get

$$Y = \frac{1}{(1-b) + \dfrac{g_1 j_1}{j_2}}\left[g_0 + a - \frac{g_1}{j_2}(u) + \frac{g_1}{j_2}(M_0)\right]$$

and therefore the change in income is given by

$$\Delta Y = \frac{1}{(1-b) + \dfrac{g_1 j_1}{j_2}}\left[\Delta g_0 + \Delta a - \frac{g_1}{j_2}(\Delta u) + \frac{g_1}{j_2}(\Delta M_0)\right]$$

Specifically we can derive the multipliers for each exogenous change from the Δ equation above. A change in investment (Δg_0) is given by

$$\Delta Y = \frac{1}{(1-b) + \dfrac{g_1 j_1}{j_2}}(\Delta g_0)$$

A change in the money supply (ΔM_0) is given by

$$\Delta Y = \frac{\dfrac{1}{(1-b)}\, j_2 + j_1}{g_1}\,(\Delta M_0)$$

A change in savings ($-\Delta a$) is given by

$$\Delta Y = \frac{1}{(1-b) + \dfrac{g_1 j_1}{j_2}}\,(-\Delta a)$$

A change in the demand for money (Δu) is given by

$$\Delta Y = \frac{\dfrac{1}{(1-b)}\, j_2 + j_1}{g_1}\,(\Delta u)$$

3

Aggregate supply in the closed economy

Our aim in this chapter is to derive the aggregate supply curve. In order to accomplish this we need to look explicitly at the production side of the economy. We do this by first considering the aggregate production function and then linking this to the labour market. In the final section of the chapter the aggregate supply and demand analyses are combined.

3.1 Aggregate supply in the short run

A production function tells us the maximum output that can be produced from given inputs of capital and labour. In the short run, the amount of capital will be fixed, and the input that can be varied quickly will be the quantity of labour. The short-run aggregate production function can therefore be simplified to a relationship between the total number of workers, referred to as labour (assuming the number of hours worked by each worker is constant), and total output, as shown in Figure 3.1. The vertical axis measures output (and real income), Y, and the horizontal axis the number of workers, L. The capital stock reflected in this short-run production function is $\bar{K}_0$.

The shape of the aggregate production function reflects diminishing marginal returns to labour – the marginal output, or product, falls as employment increases.

Now consider *the demand for labour*. Under conditions of perfect

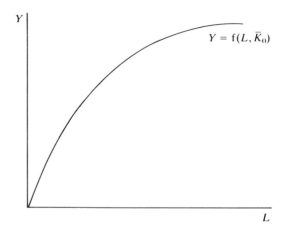

Figure 3.1 Production function showing the relation between output and labour inputs for a given capital stock

competition, employers will take on extra labour so long as the cost of the marginal worker does not exceed the extra revenue that can be obtained from the extra output the worker produces. The marginal cost is the money wage (W), the extra revenue is the marginal product of labour (MP_L) multiplied by the price at which a unit of output is sold (P). If the money wage is less than the marginal revenue product ($MP_L \cdot P$), employment is increased. But since the production function is characterised by diminishing returns, the marginal product of labour falls, and equilibrium is reached when $W = MP_L \cdot P$. If wages then fell, employment would increase once more, until $W = MP_L \cdot P$. So the demand for labour is represented by a downward-sloping curve (Figure 3.2).

So far we have stated that the condition for profit-maximising behaviour in relation to the demand for labour is

$$W = MP_L \cdot P \tag{3.1}$$

This can be arranged (and we shall see shortly why it is useful to do so) as

$$\frac{W}{P} = MP_L \tag{3.2}$$

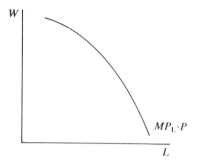

Figure 3.2 Demand for labour as a function of the wage rate

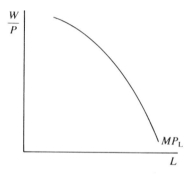

Figure 3.3 Demand for labour as a function of the real wage

This says that the condition for profit maximising is that the marginal product of labour should equal the *real* wage. We can therefore redraw the demand curve for labour as the marginal product curve, with employment as a function of the real wage (Figure 3.3).

Now consider *the supply of labour*. An increase in labour supply can come about in two ways. First, those persons already in employment may increase the number of hours they work. Second, more people may enter into employment. What would induce workers to change their supply decision? The major reason for working is to earn income which can be used in the future. It seems reasonable to suppose, therefore, that the supply of labour will depend on the real wage received. How will an increase in the real wage affect the two channels for increasing labour supply? For those already in employment, higher real wages mean an increase in the price of leisure time, but at the same time they can enjoy a higher income for the same effort. The impact on labour supply will therefore depend on the net result of these two effects, which are known as the 'substitution effect' towards work and against leisure, and the 'income effect' towards leisure and against work. The effect of higher wages on labour supply through the second channel is less ambiguous. People who were previously not willing to give up their leisure will now be prepared to enter employment at the higher wage.

In practice, when we combine these two types of individual response for the total labour force, we can expect to find that higher real wages will raise the overall supply of labour, giving an upward-sloping supply of labour curve (Figure 3.4).

We can now combine the labour demand and supply curves to derive the competitive equilibrium in the labour market (Figure 3.5). Here the economy settles at an equilibrium real wage W_0/P_0 and level of employment L_0. Both the households and the enterprises are content with this outcome – the households maximise their satisfaction from their work/leisure choice, and the firms are maximising profits. They are, in other words, on their demand and supply curves.

In this model of the labour market, if the price level rises to P_1 the

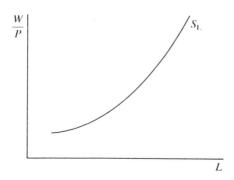

Figure 3.4   Supply of labour as a function of the real wage

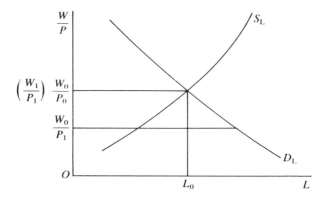

Figure 3.5   Equilibrium in the labour market with flexible wages

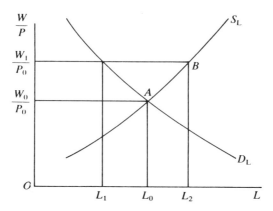

Figure 3.6   Labour market with fixed wages

real wage will fall to W_0/P_1 (i.e. $W_0/P_1 < W_0/P_0$). In this case the demand for labour exceeds the supply of labour and the money wage will be bid up to restore equilibrium at W_1/P_1, which is equivalent to the original equilibrium real wage point of W_0/P_0.

So far, analysis of the labour market has relied on supply and demand forces working in an unhampered manner. The problem with the model, called a flexible wage model, is that it does not explain unemployment: labour voluntarily chooses not to offer its services at various real wage levels. It does not explain why involuntary unemployment can occur.

An alternative approach is to postulate that the labour market will not always adjust quickly to achieve supply and demand equilibrium at L_0. To do this, the assumption that the real wage adjusts rapidly to remove any initial disequilibrium between the supply and demand for labour is dropped. If for the moment we assume a given price level, then a change in the real wage can therefore only occur through a change in the money wage. Modifying the previous model, we now assume that money wages are flexible in an upwards direction, but rigid in a downwards direction. The actual level of employment will then depend on the supply curve for labour, which is determined by the fixed money wage level and the price level, and the position of the labour demand curve which is a function of the real wage. This is in contrast to the flexible wage model where equilibrium in the labour market is independent of the price level since a change in the price level will simply lead to a change in the money wage to restore equilibrium.

In Figure 3.6, at real wage W_1/P_0, which is higher than the equilibrium real wage W_0/P_0, the supply of labour (L_2) exceeds the demand (L_1). In this case the supply of labour curve becomes OW_1/P_0BS_L instead of OW_0/P_0AS_L. Since the money wage cannot fall, there is unemployment of amount $L_2 - L_1$. Employment in this case is at L_1, being determined by the demand for labour that enterprises are willing to hire.

3.2 The aggregate supply curve

We now have a relationship between real wages and employment embodied in two models, one with flexible wages and the other with inflexible or fixed wages. The level of employment can in turn be linked to the level of output via the production function relation. This information can be represented in the form of an aggregate supply curve, which shows the amount of output which the economy will supply at different price levels. The labour market and aggregate production function are brought together in Figure 3.7 to derive the aggregate supply curve.

In the SW quadrant we have the labour market, with supply and demand of labour as functions of the real wage. The SE quadrant gives the short-run production function. If the wage rate is flexible, we know that the level of employment is determined independently

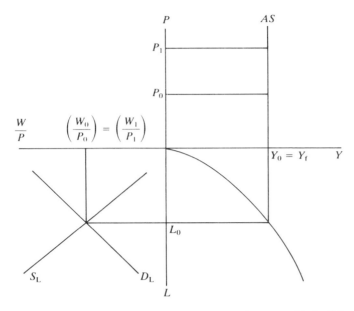

Figure 3.7 Derivation of the aggregate supply curve with flexible wages

of the price level. Suppose we begin with the real wage level W_0/P_0, which gives an employment level L_0 and an output level Y_0. Y_0 is the full employment level of output Y_f. If we now assume that the price level is P_1, in the flexible wage model the money wage will adjust to keep the real wage constant so that $(W_0/P_0) = (W_1/P_1)$. The student should note that in this case the money wage will rise to offset the fall in the real wage resulting from the rise in the price level. In this way equilibrium is preserved in the labour market and employment and output remain at L_0 and Y_0 respectively. It is easy to see from this that the aggregate supply curve shown in the NE quadrant is vertical. The supply curve is determined independently of the price level and is therefore unaffected by changes in the price level.

What happens to the aggregate supply curve in the situation where money wages are inflexible in a downward direction? In the extreme case the money wage may be fixed by institutional factors. The first point to be made is that in this framework the aggregate supply curve is derived from the demand for labour curve and the

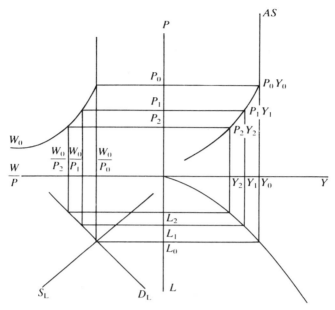

Figure 3.8 Derivation of the aggregate supply curve with fixed wages

aggregate production function: the supply curve of labour is left out. The reason is that, since the labour market does not normally achieve equilibrium in this model, we have to rely on either the demand or supply of labour relation. In the fixed wage model the aggregate supply curve depends on the demand for labour relation (i.e. the profit-maximising decisions of enterprises), and the aggregate production function.

Figure 3.8 is similar to Figure 3.7 except that we add another curve shown in the NW quadrant. This curve shows a fixed money wage throughout its length. For a fixed money wage, various points along the adjacent axes show the real wage associated with different price levels for a specific money wage.

In Figure 3.8 the real wage W_0/P_0 also represents the full employment level (equivalent to the equilibrium level in the flexible wage model). At prices higher than P_0 the aggregate supply curve is unaffected by changes in the price level and the supply curve is vertical.

Starting with the price level P_0, which corresponds to a real wage W_0/P_0 when the fixed money wage is W_0, a line can be extended through the labour market in the SW quadrant, to the production function in the SE quadrant and up to the NE quadrant. In this quadrant the points P_0 and Y_0 can be joined and indicated by P_0Y_0. This shows the level of supply producers are willing to provide when the price level is P_0. The procedure can be repeated for the other lower price levels shown in Figure 3.8, each of which increases the real wage. Finally the points in the NE quadrant can be joined together to form an aggregate supply curve. This time the curve is not vertical as was the case with the flexible wage model, but is instead upward sloping below real income level Y_0. It is also clear that the supply curve is constructed on the basis of a fixed money wage. Each time the money wage changes, a new supply curve must be constructed.

A change in the money wage is depicted in Figure 3.9. In this case the money wage is increased from W_0 to W_1, represented by an outward shift in the money wage curve shown in the NW quadrant. The effect on the aggregate supply curve can be illustrated by beginning at price P_0. With the price of P_0 the real wage associated with W_1 is W_1/P_0. As can be seen, this is higher than W_0/P_0. Tracing this line through the labour market, giving L_1, and through the production function, giving Y_1, shows that the points of interconnection between P and Y lie to the left of the original aggregate supply curve. Again this can be repeated for other price levels to form a new aggregate supply curve.

Whenever the money wage changes in the fixed money wage model (money wages inflexible downwards) the aggregate supply curve shifts. It should also be clear that the position and shape of the demand for labour function, together with the technical relation specified in the shape of the production relationship, are instrumental in determining the shape of the aggregate supply curve. The student can vary the shape of the demand for labour curve and the production function and redraw the aggregate supply curve to verify this point. A flatter demand for labour curve (demand for labour more sensitive to changes in the real wage) gives a steeper aggregate supply curve.

To reiterate, the slope of the *AS* curve is determined by the underlying conditions in the labour market. If money wages are fixed or inflexible in a downward direction, the *AS* curve is upward

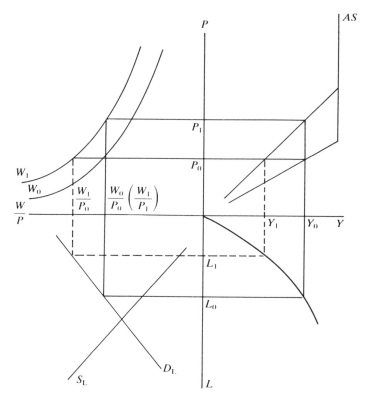

Figure 3.9 The effect of a change in the money wage on the aggregate supply curve in the fixed money wage model

sloping at levels of output below full employment. In Figure 3.8 a rise in the price level from P_2 to P_1 lowers the real wage that employers have to pay, and they therefore find it profitable to increase their output and hence their demand for labour. In this case equilibrium is achieved at P_1Y_1. It should be noted that with our inflexible money wage model the price level must rise to P_0 for full employment to be achieved. In the flexible wage model the economy is always at the full employment level. A rise in the price level which reduces the real wage will lead to a compensating rise in the money wage which leaves the real wage unchanged and the economy in full employment. The AS curve therefore depends on a different labour supply relationship from that used in the flexible

wage model. In the flexible wage model it is the assumption that the
money wage responds to a rise or fall in prices, at least in the short
run, that provides the vertical *AS* curve. Notice that we could relax
the assumption of complete downward inflexibility (below W_0) in
money wages somewhat. Provided money wages increase (fall) less
(more) rapidly than the price level rises (falls), real wages will
decline, and the *AS* curve slope upward. The slope of the *AS* curve
therefore depends on whether firms adjust to changing prices faster
than their workers.

So far we have assumed that the aggregate supply curve is derived
under conditions of perfect competition in the goods market. Firms
maximise profits by equating their marginal cost with price, and
therefore hire labour to the point where the real wage (W/P) is
equal to the marginal product of labour (MPL). The position of the
aggregate supply curve will, however, be determined to a large
extent by the degree to which the goods market is imperfect.

We can illustrate the effect of imperfect competition on the
aggregate supply curve by assuming that a small number of firms or
enterprises are able to influence domestic prices by manipulating
the quantity produced. In the case of monopoly the marginal
revenue is less than the price so that the profit-maximising condition
becomes $W/P = (MR/P) MPL$. This means that the demand for
labour curve will lie to the left of the curve illustrated in Figure 3.5.

The aggregate supply curve under imperfectly competitive market conditions can be worked out using Figure 3.8. Draw a new
demand for labour curve $D_L{}^1$ which lies to the right of the original
curve D_L. Redraw the *AS* curve using the various real wage levels
W_0/P_0, W_0/P_1 and W_0/P_2. This time the *AS* curve will lie to the left
of the original curve derived under perfectly competitive market
conditions. Imperfect competition does not change the vertical part
of the curve.

We can now summarise what has been said about the aggregate
supply curve. We began with the flexible wage model and saw that,
if nominal wages are fully flexible, we will have a vertical aggregate
supply curve at full employment. If money wages are not fully
flexible, the aggregate supply is upward sloping below the full
employment level. The crucial question, therefore, is how do wages
behave in practice. This is ultimately an empirical question which
can be resolved only by considering the evidence for a particular
economy. The slope of the aggregate supply curve is of crucial

importance for macroeconomic policy, especially demand management policy. If the aggregate supply curve is upward sloping, it will be possible to vary the level of output and employment (at the same time raising the price level) by increasing the level of aggregate demand. But if the AS curve is vertical, an increase in aggregate demand will simply increase the price level.

3.3 The aggregate demand and supply framework and macro policy

Most economists argue that, in the short run, the AS curve will be upward sloping, but over time it will begin to shift towards the vertical, as wages become more flexible and responsive to changes in the price level. In this section we therefore bring together the upward sloping AS curve and the downward sloping AD curve to create a simple model of the whole economy. It must be remembered at this stage that we have been analysing the components of aggregate supply in isolation from aggregate demand. It should also be clear that we are about to drop the assumption made throughout Chapter 2 that output will always change whenever desired expenditures change. We have now specified that output is determined by conditions in the labour market and technology. By combining the conditions for supply and demand we can explicitly introduce the price level as an *endogenous* rather than an *exogenous* variable, and discuss in detail the way in which the price level achieves equilibrium.

The AS and AD curves summarise underlying activity in the markets for goods, money and labour. To understand how the model works we need to trace through the effects on these markets. In Figure 3.10 aggregate demand is raised from AD_1 to AD_2. Suppose this is the result of an exogenous increase in investment expenditure by the government. In Figure 3.11 this is shown by a rightward shift in the IS curve from IS_1 to IS_2, disturbing the equilibrium in the goods market, r_1Y_1. Initially, this additional expenditure will increase income to Y_2. But the higher transactions demand for money will cause the interest rate to rise to r_3, with output falling to Y_3 and equilibrium being restored in the goods and money markets. The Y_3 in Figure 3.11 is the same as the Y_3 in Figure 3.10. However, from Figure 3.10 we can see that, although the demand side of the economy is in equilibrium, the economy is not in overall equilibrium since AD is greater than AS. In this situation the price level begins to rise and the economy begins to move towards an equilibrium at P_4Y_4, causing further adjustments to occur in the markets underlying the aggregate curves.

In the money market, the rise in the price level reduces the money supply value in real terms, causing the LM curve to shift to $LM_0(P_4)$ in Figure 3.11. This raises the interest rate to r_4, which reduces investment demand with output demand shifting along the IS_2 curve to Y_4. The equilibrium income level Y_4 in Figure 3.10 corresponds with Y_4 in Figure 3.11.

In the labour market, higher prices cause the real wage to fall, and the demand for labour increases along the demand for labour curve (not shown). This increases the level of output supplied, which in terms of Figure 3.10 is seen as a movement along the AS curve.

Although for most of the book we will be analysing policy using the aggregate supply and demand framework, it is useful to trace the results of changes to the variables using the components that are synthesised in the aggregate demand and supply curves. Consider, for example, the effect of a change in government expenditure, using the four quadrant diagram. Here the changes seen in Figure 3.10 are shown in the NE quadrant of Figure 3.12 and those in Figure 3.11 in the SE quadrant. A new relationship is introduced in the NW quadrant. This is constructed in a similar manner to the derivation of the aggregate demand (AD) curve. It was shown earlier in Figure 2.10 that a relationship exists between the rate of interest and the price level, such that in Figure 2.10 r_1 was associated with P_0, r_2 with P_1, and so on. The relationship in the NW quadrant of Figure 3.12 shows the effect on interest rates arising from changes in the real supply of money as changes in aggregate demand (i.e. changes in investment, consumption, government expenditure and the nominal supply of money) raise or lower the price level.

In Figure 3.12 the increase in government expenditure shifts the IS curve from IS_1 to IS_2 and the AD curve from AD_1 to AD_2. The RR curve also shifts in the opposite direction to the AD curve. (The student should compare this with a change originating in the LM curve, which will shift the RR curve in the same direction as the change in the AD curve.) Changes in interest rates resulting from

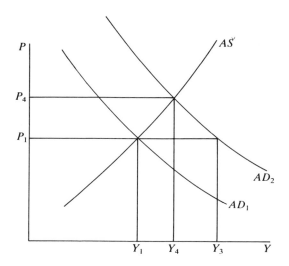

Figure 3.10   An increase in aggregate demand

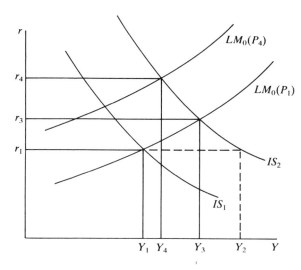

Figure 3.11   The effect of a shift in the *IS* curve when the price level is variable

price level changes are shown by shifts in the *LM* curve in the SE
quadrant and by movements along the *RR* curve in the NW
quadrant (the direction indicated by arrows). The NW quadrant in
Figure 3.12 can therefore be used to show the effect that changes in
nominal aggregate demand have on the rate of interest (shown by
shifts in the *RR* curve) and changes in the price level that affect
interest rates (shown by movements along the *RR* curve).

The workings on the supply side can be similarly shown with the
aid of Figure 3.13, which combines the labour market and
production function. It can be seen that a shift in aggregate demand
arising from a change in government investment expenditure raises
income, employment and the price level. Within the context of the
fixed wage model, the real wage falls, resulting in a movement along

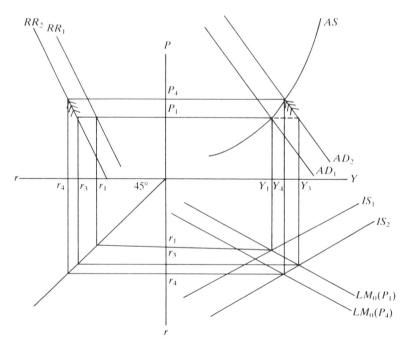

Figure 3.12   The effect of an increase in aggregate demand on the *AD*, *IS*,
LM and *RR* curves

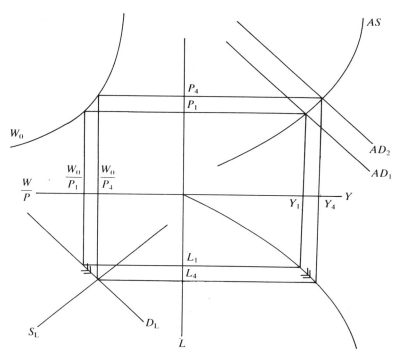

Figure 3.13 The effect of an increase in aggregate demand on the labour market and the production function

the demand for labour curve and the production function indicated by the arrows.

Will the equilibrium at P_4Y_4 be stable in the long run? We have seen that the upward-sloping aggregate supply curve depends on the fall in real wages, caused by a rise in prices and unchanged money wages. If labour begins to react to the decline in its real wage by reducing its supply, then the AS curve will move towards a vertical position. If this happens, the final result of the initial increase in investment expenditure will be an increase in the overall price level, but no change in the level of output. The effectiveness of the demand stimulus in raising output and employment therefore depends on the response (or lack of response) of labour to a reduction in real wages. We take up this issue again in Chapter 9, where the response of labour to a decline in real wages is ᵗ ᵗ seek higher money wages.

Further reading

Further detail on the diagrammatic treatment of some of the relationships described in this chapter can be found in Smith (1966). See also Grossman and Barro (1976) for the working of the fixed wage model, and Taylor (1979) for an analysis that incorporates expectations into the derivation of the aggregate supply curve. Labour market conditions in developing countries are discussed in Squire (1981) and McDiarmid (1977).

4

Money supply and the financial sector

Money can be defined as a highly liquid asset. 'Liquidity' relates to the ready convertibility of money into goods and services. Money is therefore an asset which can be conveniently used as a medium of exchange. An 'asset' is also a means of holding wealth, and money can be used for this purpose although in the form of notes and coins it will yield no financial return.

There are varying degrees of liquidity and consequently the identification of the assets which can be categorised as money can vary. The narrowest definition of money, and the one on which there is general agreement, is currency (notes and coins) and current account bank deposits held by the public. This definition is referred to as M1.

In most countries the central monetary authority, usually the Central Bank, is responsible for issuing the currency. In many developing countries this was the responsibility of the Currency Board in the pre-independence period. The suppliers of current account deposits, in the main, are the commercial banks. Some of these are in public ownership, which means they do not always operate to maximise profits.

In this chapter we shall consider how the Central Bank controls the money supply. Initially we assume a closed economy, in which case the money supply is equivalent to

$$SM = C_u + B_D + D \tag{4.1}$$

where SM represents the money supply,

C_u is currency in the economy,

B_D are bankers' deposits held at the Central Bank,

D is the amount of commercial bank deposits.

C_u and B_D form the monetary base since they are completely substitutable.

The money supply changes through changes in the monetary base or high-powered money, as it is otherwise known, and through the credit creation process of the commercial banks. In many developing countries the stock of high-powered money has grown enormously, with the Central Bank providing currency to the government in exchange for government debt. This has increased the money supply through the increase in currency in circulation. However, by far the more important source of increased money supply in most countries is the growth resulting from the creation of commercial bank deposits. We therefore need to give attention to these two aspects of the money supply. We first consider the deposit creation process of the commercial banks.

4.1 Deposit creation

Practices in banking and the relationships between the Central Bank and commercial banks will differ between countries. However, most banking systems operate on a partial reserve system, where the commercial banks are legally required to hold a certain proportion of their deposits in the form of high-powered money, or reserve assets as they are otherwise referred to. Since the Central Bank controls the supply of high-powered money, it can also to a large extent control the deposit-creating capacity of the commercial banks, and hence the total money supply.

What is important to the commercial banks, therefore, is the total amount of these reserve assets made available to the economy (i.e. supplied by the Central Bank), and the proportion that passes into the commercial banking system. This will, of course, depend on the behaviour of the private non-banking sector, consisting of households and enterprises, in depositing their holdings of currency in the commercial banks. The deposit-creating ability of the commercial banks is therefore set by the level of their holdings of reserve assets and the legally imposed ratio of reserves to deposits.

The deposit-creating process of the commercial banks can be simply illustrated. Table 4.1 provides the balance sheets of two of the principal agents that determine the size of deposit creation, the private non-bank sector (B) and the commercial banks (C). The other agent shown without a balance sheet is the Central Bank (A). Deposit creation is shown by the Central Bank initially supplying currency (base money) to the private non-bank sector, which in turn deposits the currency with the banks by opening current accounts. Credit creation commences when the banks receive deposits.

In order to explain the sequence of the process shown in Table 4.1 a number of simplifying assumptions will be made. We will first assume that the private non-bank sector receives the high-powered money directly, as opposed to having it filtered through the banking system or by buying bonds from the non-bank sector. Second, we assume that the non-bank sector deposits all the money it receives in the commercial banks. Third, we assume that the commercial banks will want to use all the currency made available to them apart from the reserves they are legally required to hold. The reserve requirement against deposits (the reserve ratio) is established by the central authorities at 10 per cent.

In Step 1 the Central Bank prints £200 of high-powered money or reserve assets in the form of currency. In Step 2 it passes these to the non-bank private sector, which in Step 3 opens deposits in the commercial bank sector. This transfers the £200 asset held in currency in the non-bank sector to the banking sector. It remains an asset for the non-bank sector, although its form has changed from an asset measured in currency to one held as a deposit. Similarly, the banks now have an asset in currency. They also have a liability in the form of a deposit since individuals in the non-bank sector have the right to withdraw their currency from the banks.

The banks are now in a position to lend on the basis of their accumulated assets. This is done in Step 4 when the banks lend to the non-bank sector. The banks create a loan of £180 from the £200 assets they hold in currency, keeping £20 (or 10 per cent) as a reserve against deposits. The non-bank sector in Step 4 now has currency as an asset and a bank loan as a liabiity. Notice in Step 4 that the loan becomes an asset for the banks.

In Step 5 the non-bank sector again deposits the currency from the loan into the banks, and the banks in turn (Step 6) use it, less the legally stipulated reserve requirement, to create another loan,

Table 4.1 The deposit-creating process (£s)

	Step 1	Step 2	Step 3	Step 4	Step 5	Step 6	Step 7	Step 8
Central Bank (A)								
Assets	200							
Non-bank financial sector (B)								
Assets								
Currency	–	200	–	180		144		115.2
Deposits	–	–	200		180		144	
Liabilities								
Loans	–	–		180		144		115.2
Commercial banks (C)								
Assets								
Currency	–	–		20		36		28.8
Loans	–	–	200	180	180	144	144	115.2
Liabilities								
Deposits	–	–	200		180		144	

this time amounting to £144. The process continues in subsequent steps until the amounts for lending become infinitely small.

What has happened to the money supply in this process? Remember it consists of currency and deposits. We began with a money base of £200 in Step 1. By Step 4 it had grown to £380 (£200 + £180) and by Step 6 to £524 (£200 + £180 + £144). It continues until the asset row for the non-bank sector equals £2,000, so that deposit creation has extended the money supply by ten times its base level.

In terms of Table 4.1 deposit creation becomes

$$D = (C_u - C_p) 1/R \tag{4.2}$$

where D is the quantity of commercial bank deposits,

C_u is the amount of currency,

C_p is the currency held by the private non-bank sector outside the banks,

$1/R$ is the reserve ratio, expressed as a fraction of deposits.

The reserve ratio expresses the fraction of reserve assets that are legally required to be held back by the commercial banks. They cannot use this fraction for commercial purposes either to create loans or to buy bonds. In our example, C_u is equal to £200, being the quantity of currency the Central Bank originally issued to the system. C_p is zero since we assumed that the non-bank financial sector does not want to hold currency outside the banks. $1/R$ is 10 per cent. Substituting these values in equation 4.2 gives a level of deposit creation of £2,000. This results from an original injection of base money of £200. This figure represents the money supply since this is defined as notes and coins (currency) in circulation and deposits, which in the simplified example in Table 4.1, and after the deposit creation process, have a value of £2,000.

The process just illustrated can be expressed in a slightly different way incorporating the commercial bank deposits held at the Central Bank. The equation for deposit creation then becomes

$$D = (C_u + B_D - C_p) 1/R \tag{4.3}$$

where B_D = bankers' deposits held at the Central Bank.

Deposit creation, therefore, depends on the quantity of the reserve assets (currency) made available to the banks. If all the currency issued is deposited in the commercial banks, then the banks can expand deposit creation to the maximum permitted by the constraints of the legally imposed reserve requirement $(1/R)$. Of obvious importance for the deposit-creating process is the part of currency that is kept outside of the banking system.

Since the term C_p concerns the behaviour of the private non-bank sector and represents its holdings of the reserve assets or currency held outside the banks, it can also be expressed as a fraction of the sector's deposits that are held in the banks (cD). The expression for deposit creation can be rewritten as

$$D = (C_u + B_D - cD)\,1/R$$

In this case D refers to the quantity of deposits and c to the coefficient showing the fraction of deposits held outside the banks in the form of currency.

So far, we have looked in a simplified manner at the way in which the banking sector engages in the process of deposit creation. The total money supply picture can now be restated. Recall that the money supply was defined as currency held by the private non-bank sector (cD) and the deposits in banks (D). The money supply then becomes

$$SM = C_p + D \tag{4.4}$$

and

$$C_p = cD \tag{4.5}$$

therefore

$$SM = D(c + 1) \tag{4.6}$$

Also since $D = (C_u + B_D - cD)\,1/R$ then

$$D(R + c) = C_u + B_D \tag{4.7}$$

and

$$D = \frac{1}{(R + c)}[C_u + B_D] \tag{4.8}$$

The money supply then becomes

$$SM = \frac{c + 1}{c + R}(C_u + B_D) \tag{4.9}$$

where $c + 1/c + R$ is defined as the money multiplier m. A condensed equation for the money supply then becomes

$$SM = m(C_u + B_D) \qquad (4.10)$$

We have therefore shown the money supply process in a closed economy to be determined by the quantity of reserve assets (currency) issued by the Central Bank and the deposit creation ability of the commercial banks. Their ability to create credit was in turn constrained by the amount of currency held outside the banking sector and the legally imposed reserve requirements on deposits. In this system the Central Bank can control the money supply by changing the money base and through its control over the reserve requirements of the commercial banks.

At this stage, a few numerical examples will help the reader to understand how the control of the money supply works. Suppose the money base is £200, the reserve ratio is 10 per cent and the non-bank private sector keeps 10 per cent of the quantity of currency it receives outside the banking sector. Substituting in equation (4.9) gives

$$SM = \frac{0.1 + 1}{0.1 + 0.1} [£200]$$

which produces a total money supply of £1,100. Money held 'outside' the banks can be calculated by subtracting money created through deposit creation (often referred to as 'inside money'). This is given by equation (4.8) so that

$$D = \frac{1}{0.1 + 0.1} [£200] = £1,000$$

We can calculate the impact of a change in the reserve requirement from 10 per cent to 20 per cent on total money supply, again using equation (4.9):

$$SM = \frac{0.1 + 1}{0.1 + 0.2} [£200] = £733.30$$

This time the money supply is reduced. Finally, a change in the money base from £200 to £300 raises the money supply to £1,650 when the reserve ratio is 10 per cent and to £1,100 when the ratio is 20 per cent.

4.2 Government and the money sector

We are now in a position to re-examine the money sector with the inclusion of government. Earlier we stated that in the money supply process we were interested in the behaviour of three agents, the Central Bank, the commercial banks and the private sector (non-banks).

The Central Bank controlled the issue of currency. The commercial banks, through the deposit system, had the power to create credit. The private sector restricted the credit-creating ability of banks by not making available all reserve assets (currency) to the banking system.

The commercial banks are required to hold deposits at the Central Bank (B_D). In economies where some form of capital market exists, the Central Bank is able to influence the money supply by buying and selling bonds from either the commercial banks or the private sector. This process is known as open market operations. The Central Bank can sell bonds to the private sector. In return the individuals in the private sector present cheques written on their accounts in the commercial banks. The Central Bank then debits the accounts of the commercial banks held at the Central Bank. Since no other account in the banking system is credited, the commercial banks' deposits balance held at the Central Bank goes down. The fall in the commercial banks' reserve asset holdings forces them to reduce the level of deposits, thereby causing the money supply to fall. In this case B_D goes down and C_u remains unchanged, but the money supply falls since it depends on B_D and C_u.

To this scheme we now add a fourth agent, the government. Introducing government adds another dimension to the Central Bank's activities. It is no longer simply a banker to the commercial banks, but now also acts as banker to the government. The government can finance its expenditure in a number of ways – via taxation or by borrowing. These must now be explained in relation to the money supply. Assume that the government is unable to finance an increase in expenditure by increased taxation. It can now do three things: borrow from the Central Bank; borrow from the commercial banks; or borrow from the private sector. Let us consider each of these options in turn, assuming that the government starts from a balanced budget ($G = T$) situation, and wants to increase its expenditure.

Borrowing from the Central Bank

The Central Bank acts as banker to the government and it therefore does for the government what commercial banks do for the public, i.e. it provides advances. Often the advances are required to finance the day-to-day activities of the government because the flow of revenues does not match expenditures. The government also borrows long term from the Central Bank for its investment programme.

Financing expenditure by borrowing from the Central Bank raises the domestic money supply. In this process, the balance sheet of the Central Bank shows an increase in its assets, in the form of claims on the government and on the liability side in the form of government deposits and currency. The government, by making payments for goods and services, is able to increase the suppliers' deposits and currency holdings. Of course, the actual impact on the total money supply will be subject to the size of the money multiplier. This can be predicted by accurately measuring the components of the multiplier, assuming the various behavioural coefficients are stable.

Borrowing from the commercial banks

If the government's budget deficit is financed in this way, the monetary effects will depend upon the behaviour of the banks. If the banks' excess reserves are zero (or a constant proportion of bank deposits) then the commercial banks can lend to the government only at the cost of their credit to the private sector. In this case there will be no change in the money supply. On the other hand, it is often possible for the commercial banks to increase their lending to the government without reducing their credit to the private sector, in which case it will affect the money supply. This is accomplished if the Central Bank is willing to expand the supply of reserve assets to commercial banks, or if the commercial banks themselves hold excess reserves. This can either take place through open market operations or by increasing discounts and advances to banks (we return to this in Chapter 7).

The question might be asked why reserve assets might be increased to commercial banks. Several explanations are possible. An increase in the Central Bank's supply of reserve assets to the commercial banks might be due to pressure exerted by the commercial banks, the government or the Central Bank itself to moderate the effects that government borrowing might have on interest rates or on the supply of credit to the rest of the economy. If the reserve assets are increased to the commercial banks, however, such an approach is tantamount to the government debt being financed ultimately by the Central Bank, as it involves a policy decision to intervene in the relation between government borrowing and commercial bank lending.

Borrowing from the private sector

Borrowing from the private sector transfers resources from the private sector to the government sector. It does not reduce total wealth. Lending of this kind is usually voluntary, taking place in some form of financial market. Government bonds or securities paying interest are issued to individuals in the private sector, with the interest rate paid varying according to the liquidity of the debt instrument. For example, a bond issued for a short term will pay a lower interest rate than one issued with a longer-term maturity. A large proportion of non-bank lending to government is undertaken by insurance companies, pension funds and provident funds, which are often referred to as captive lenders.

Borrowing from the private sector does not directly lead to a change in the money supply. Its primary effect is to displace private consumption and investment. The actual effect will depend upon the types of instrument issued to the private sector to finance the debt. Long-term bonds, representing assets with a low liquidity and high yields, will be more effective in displacing private expenditure than short-term instruments. This is because holders of long-term bonds, although they can sell them to redeem cash, would be subject to greater risks of loss since the market price of long-term bonds tends to fluctuate more than that of short-term bonds.

We have now examined the three ways in which the government may finance a budget deficit. Although the most prevalent means is to borrow from the Central Bank, creating an immediate expansion in money supply, the other types of borrowing may also be used. It would be incorrect, therefore, to equate the budget deficit with

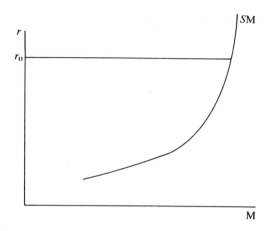

Figure 4.1 Upward-sloping supply of money function

high-powered reserves and to incorporate it directly into the money supply base so long as the government has a choice over the size of the budget deficit and its means of finance. The difficulty in controlling the size of the budget deficit, particularly during an inflationary period, is discussed in Chapter 9.

The money supply curve shown in Figure 4.1 is upward sloping from left to right and eventually becomes vertical above interest rate r_0. The vertical portion of this curve represents the money supply derived from equation (4.10) when the commercial banks use all their reserve assets, except those they are legally required to hold back, for credit creation. Banks can, however, hold reserves in excess of the requirement stipulated by the Central Bank. Many banks hold excess reserves to meet the demands for cash arising from a sudden rush of customers wishing to make withdrawals. Obviously there is an opportunity cost to holding reserves, and this is reflected in the interest rate. If interest rates are low, there will be a greater tendency on the part of banks to hold excess reserves. This tendency is reflected in the money supply curve below rate of interest r_0.

A change in the rate of interest can lead to a change in the money supply for a given level of monetary base by moving along *SM*. A change in the interest rate cannot shift the *SM* curve.

4.3 Money supply in the open economy

The money supply in the open economy is affected by a change in the level of foreign exchange reserves. Under a system of fixed exchange rates, a balance of payments deficit will lead to a fall in the country's foreign exchange reserves, which in turn will cause a decline in the money supply.

In order to see how this works we need to look at the balance sheet of the Central Bank in the same way that we examined the balance sheet of commercial banks in an earlier section. In the open economy the Central Bank's assets consist of a component of domestic credit and the holdings of foreign exchange reserves and gold (R). The Central Bank's holdings of each may be held in other central banks around the world, usually in the form of some type of security that is highly liquid in terms of foreign currencies. The domestic credit represents the bonds that are purchased from government when currency is put into circulation. This was the only type of asset held in the Central Bank when we assumed a closed economy. The liability side of the Central Bank's balance sheet consists as before of the money base or currency that is issued. In the closed economy the Central Bank controlled the money supply through changes in the level of domestic credit. In terms of the open economy, the Central Bank's assets include R, the holdings of gold and foreign exchange reserves. A change in the money supply occurs in the open economy through a change in either domestic credit or reserves.

Does the Central Bank have control over both? If the government wants to maintain a fixed exchange, the answer is a qualified no. It clearly can control the level of domestic credit through its control over the money base and the reserve ratio. It changes the amount of currency in circulation in a variety of ways discussed earlier in this chapter. However, in the case of an open economy with a fixed exchange rate, the ability to control the total money supply is less evident. The Central Bank will use its stock of foreign exchange reserves in order to maintain the desired level of exchange rate (as we show in Chapter 8, if a balance of payments deficit is not financed by a rundown of foreign exchange reserves, the exchange rate itself will change). The monetary base is therefore changed as the level of foreign reserves is altered. As before, the effect on the total money supply is still determined by the size of the money multiplier, which now becomes

$$SM = m(C_u + B_D + R) \tag{4.11}$$

The Central Bank could try to offset the effect of a change in foreign reserves on the money supply. This is generally known as 'sterilisation', and entails the Central Bank buying or selling an amount of government debt equivalent to the change in reserves. Suppose, for example, that the money supply increases as a result of increased foreign exchange earnings that produce a balance of payments surplus. In this case, in order to sterilise the effect on the money supply, the Central Bank would have to sell government bonds to claim back the increase in high-powered money in payment for the bonds. The total money supply would then remain unchanged, although the composition of the reserve asset base would have altered.

In the case of a balance of payments deficit, the Central Bank will lower the level of its foreign reserves in order to maintain the fixed exchange rate. The effect on the domestic money supply, which will be contracting in this case, can be sterilised by using the proceeds from the sale of foreign exchange to buy government bonds from the private sector. This is equivalent to increasing the domestic money supply. For sterilisation to be effective there must be a market for bonds and a sufficient level of foreign exchange reserves. Obviously it will be easier for a country with a balance of payments surplus to sterilise because its foreign exchange reserves will be rising. If a country's foreign exchange reserves are low and it faces a balance of payments deficit, then alternative action may need to be considered (see Chapter 8).

Further reading

A useful summary of an industrialised country's banking arrangements is contained in National Westminster Bank (1985). For developing countries the reader is referred to McKinnon (1973), Shaw (1973) and the more recent work of Fry (1988). Useful articles are also contained in World Development (1982).

5

Demand and supply in the open economy

In this chapter the basic model is extended to incorporate the effects of international trade and capital flows. International trade arises from transactions of goods and services between countries. Goods and services produced domestically are required by residents overseas (exports) just as goods and services produced elsewhere are consumed at home (imports). Similarly, residents overseas lend to, and borrow from, residents at home, giving rise to capital inflows and outflows. Incorporating international flows of capital and goods and services into the basic model changes the specification of aggregate demand and supply.

5.1   Balance of payments equilibrium

To reiterate, the balance of payments consists of the financial flows associated with the international trade in goods and services and the international movement of capital. The balance of payments (BP) can be written as

$$BP = F_t + F_c$$

where F_t and F_c are the net flows of goods and services, and of capital, respectively. If we define a balance of payments equilibrium as $BP = 0$, then to achieve equilibrium, a balance of trade surplus (deficit) must be offset by a capital account deficit (surplus). If the balance of payments is not in equilibrium, there is a change in the level of the country's foreign currency reserves. For example, if the balance of payments is in deficit ($BP < 0$), the outflow of foreign payments to overseas must exceed the inflow of payments from abroad, and the country's reserves are therefore declining. Alternatively, a country's foreign currency reserves will be rising when there is a balance of payments surplus.

5.2 Balance of trade and domestic absorption

The difference between the value of imports and the value of exports represents the economy's balance of trade. If the value of imports exceeds the value of exports, there is a deficit in the balance of trade. Net foreign demand is given by exports minus imports. In the open economy, the expression for aggregate expenditure on domestically produced goods becomes $C + I + G + (X - M)$. Total expenditure is equal *ex post* to national income, i.e.

$$Y = C + I + G + (X - M) \tag{5.1}$$

Equation (5.1) can be split into domestic and external components. Expenditure on goods by residents of the domestic economy is $C + I + G$, which is known as domestic absorption (A). $X - M$ is the trade account balance (BT). Income can therefore be written as

$$Y = A + BT$$

If $BT = 0$, then domestic income (Y) is equal to domestic expenditure (A). When $BT < 0$, the balance of trade is in deficit, domestic absorption is greater than income, and residents in the domestic economy are able to consume more than they produce.

5.3 The determinants of imports and exports

In the short run it can be hypothesised that the demand for imports is determined by the level of real income in an economy and the prices of domestic goods and services relative to the prices of goods and services produced abroad.

The relationship between imports and income is likely to be positive: as income grows, the demand for imports increases. In the case of prices, it is assumed for the time being that, since imports are substitutes for domestic goods, imports will be positively related to an increase in the domestic price level relative to the price level in the rest of the world. This means that, if we hold prices in the rest of the world constant and raise the domestic price of import substitutes so that the relative price ratio is increased, the demand for imports increases. The extent to which import demand is responsive to changes in relative prices will depend on the degree of substitution between domestic and foreign goods.

Exports are assumed to be determined by the growth of income in the rest of the world and by changes in the domestic price level relative to prices in the rest of the world. In the former case the relationship is positive: increased world income increases the demand for a country's exports. In the latter case the relationship is negative: the higher the domestic price level relative to the foreign price level, the lower will be the rest of the world's demand for the country's exports.

5.4   Capital account

The capital account of the balance of payments consists of private and official capital flows. Foreign capital flows depend mainly on the level of the domestic rate of interest relative to rates in the rest of the world. The lower the rate of interest in the domestic economy relative to rates elsewhere, the greater will be the tendency for domestic capital to flow abroad and the less will be the tendency for foreign capital to flow into the domestic economy. This is shown in Figure 5.1, where an increase in the domestic interest rate (r) relative to the rest of the world interest rate (r_w) causes an increase in the net inflow of capital (F_c).

5.5   Equilibrium in the open economy

In Chapter 3 we examined the conditions necessary to achieve internal equilibrium. For the open economy we have seen that external equilibrium requires the balance of payments to be zero.

There are important linkages between the internal and external parts of the economy. We have indicated that the external balance is influenced by the level of income and interest rates set in the

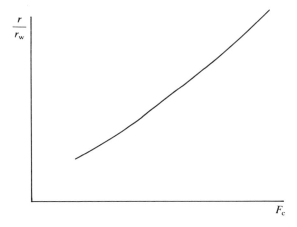

Figure 5.1 Net inflow of capital

domestic economy. Similarly, we have shown that the *IS* curve is affected by changes in aggregate expenditure originating in the trade balance. It is intuitively obvious, therefore, that we have to consider how the economy can simultaneously reach both internal and external equilibrium.

For the moment we assume that the price level is constant: in other words, the level of output is below the full capacity level and the aggregate supply curve is horizontal. We can now derive a new equilibrium curve, the *BP* line, which represents combinations of interest rate and output levels at which the balance of payments is in equilibrium. Any point along the *BP* curve represents a balance of payments equal to zero. The *BP* curve is shown in Figure 5.2.

The *BP* curve is upward sloping from left to right, indicating that a rise in domestic income worsens the trade account and that as a result a higher interest rate is required to attract an inflow of capital from abroad to match the trade deficit. Points to the left and above the *BP* line are points of balance of payments surplus; those below and to the right represent overall deficit situations. If the actual rate of interest and the income level are situated in the lower segment, such as point *A*, foreign reserves will be decreasing. At point *B* the reserve level is increasing. When we draw the *BP* curve we are assuming that the determinants of trade and capital flows, other than domestic income and interest rates, are constant. In other

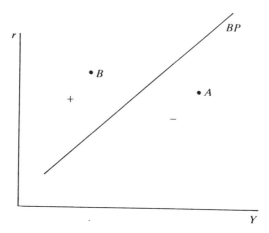

Figure 5.2   Balance of payments curve showing combinations of interest rates and income levels that give equilibrium

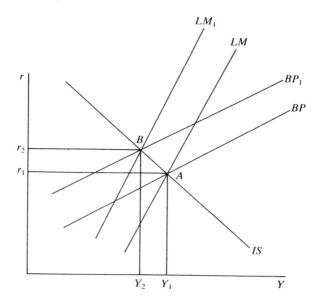

Figure 5.3   The effect of a rise in foreign interest rates

words, foreign income, foreign prices, foreign interest rates, the domestic price level and the exchange rate all remain unchanged. A change in any of these factors would shift the *BP* curve to the left or to the right.

In Figure 5.3 we have added the international sector to the goods and money sectors. Each is in equilibrium at income level Y_1 and interest rate r_1, with the *IS*, *LM* and *BP* curves intersecting at point *A*.

To see how the open economy model responds to a disturbance of an initial equilibrium, consider the following example. Let the *BP* curve shift to BP_1 as a result, say, of a rise in the foreign interest rate.[1] The *IS* and *LM* curves now intersect to the right of and below BP_1, so the level Y_1 is now associated with a balance of payments deficit. In Chapter 4 we saw how a loss of foreign reserves will lead to a reduction in the supply of money. This shifts the *LM* curve in Figure 5.3 to the left, and this will continue until the new LM_1 curve intersects the BP_1 and *IS* curves, at *B*. Internal and external equilibrium is restored at income level Y_2 and interest rate r_2.

As a second illustration, consider what happens if there is an increase in foreign income. This shifts the *BP* curve to the right (exports are now higher at every level of domestic income, and equilibrium therefore requires a lower interest rate and level of capital inflow), shown as BP_1 in Figure 5.4.

At the same time, the increase in exports adds to total expenditure and shifts the *IS* curve rightwards to IS_1. Initially, the economy moves from *A* to *B*, where the *LM* and the new *IS* curves intersect. But this is associated with a balance of payments surplus which causes the money supply to rise, shifting the *LM* curve rightwards to LM_1. Eventually equilibrium is reached at *C*, where the interest rate is lower and the level of income higher than in the original equilibrium.

5.6 Fiscal and monetary policy

So far in discussing the open economy equilibrium, we have analysed how the system will react to an exogenous 'disturbance'. It is quite possible, however, that internal and external equilibrium may be at a level of output which is below the target, full capacity level. In this case, the government may decide to use monetary

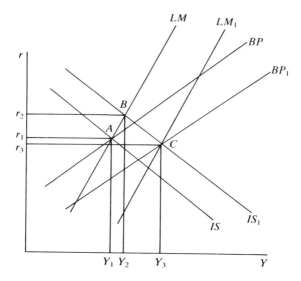

Figure 5.4   The effect of an increase in the level of foreign income

and/or fiscal policy in an attempt to raise the level of national income. How effective will these policy measures be in the open economy?

In Figure 5.5 internal and external equilibrium is at A, but the equilibrium income level Y_1 is below the full capacity level. Suppose the authorities decide to use monetary policy to increase the level of income. An increase in the quantity of money moves the LM curve to the right. But the new LM_1 curve now cuts the IS curve to the right of the BP curve at point B, which means that a balance of payments deficit has opened up. The loss of reserves will in turn lower money supply, and will shift the LM curve back to its original position. Therefore, in an open economy with fixed prices and a fixed exchange rate, monetary policy is ineffective in achieving an increase in income for more than a transition period.

Will fiscal policy be more successful? The answer is yes, and the reason is shown in Figure 5.6. An increase in government expenditure will shift the IS curve rightwards to IS_1. The new internal equilibrium is at B, with a higher income level. However, at B there is a balance of payments surplus. This leads to an inflow of reserves which shifts the LM curve rightwards to LM_1. Internal and external

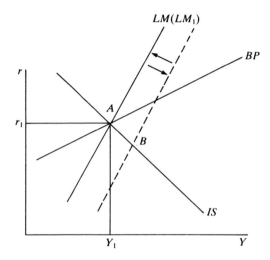

Figure 5.5 The effect of monetary policy on internal and external equilibrium

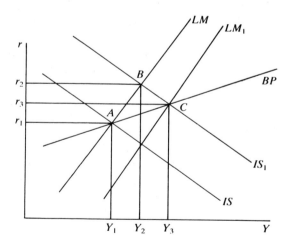

Figure 5.6 The effect of fiscal policy on internal and external equilibrium

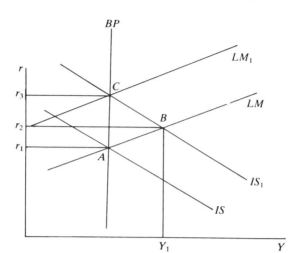

Figure 5.7 Monetary and fiscal policy when capital flows are unresponsive to changes in relative interest rates

equilibrium is achieved at C, with income raised to the higher, target level.

So far we have assumed that the BP curve is upward sloping, showing that a deterioration in the trade balance can be offset by an increased inflow of foreign capital, attracted by a higher domestic rate of interest. However, if capital movements are unresponsive to changes in interest rates, the BP curve will become vertical.

In Figure 5.7 the economy is initially in equilibrium at A. An increase in government expenditure shifts the IS curve to IS_1. The new point of intersection of LM and IS_1 is at B, which is associated with a balance of payments deficit. The decline in reserves shifts the LM curve back to LM_1 with a new equilibrium at C. Fiscal policy has been unsuccessful in raising the level of income. Monetary policy is just as ineffective in altering the equilibrium level of income when the BP curve is vertical. An increase in money supply shifts the LM curve to the right. This can be illustrated by starting at point C in Figure 5.7 and moving the LM curve from LM_1 to LM along IS_1. A balance of payments deficit emerges at point B and leads to reserve losses, which lower the LM curve back to its original position.

The only way to raise the income level and maintain internal and external equilibrium when the *BP* curve is vertical is to shift the *BP* curve to the right. This will involve an improvement either in the trade balance associated with each income level – exports must be raised and/or imports reduced – or an increase in the inflow of capital not associated with a change in relative rates of interest.

In many developing countries, capital movements in response to changes in interest rates are insignificant, and the *BP* curve is likely to be almost vertical. Much of the analysis of balance of payments adjustment in developing countries concentrates, therefore, on the trade account.

5.7 The external sector and the price level

In the preceding analysis of the international sector, the price level was ignored by assuming that it remained constant. If this assumption is removed, both the *IS* curve and the *LM* curve will shift when the price level changes. The *LM* curve shifts, as we saw in Chapter 2, as changes in the price level affect the real supply of money. The *IS* curve will shift whenever the price level changes because we have incorporated the balance of trade into the *IS* framework.

A rise in the domestic price level, holding the rest of the world price level constant, will worsen the balance of trade position. This is because a rise in domestic prices will make exports relatively more expensive to overseas customers and imports relatively cheaper to domestic buyers. Since imports and exports are components of aggregate demand and are affected by price changes, there will be a specific *IS* curve for each price level. A higher price level is associated with a lower *IS* curve. This is illustrated in Figure 5.8.

What effect will this have on the aggregate demand curve derived in Chapter 2? You will remember that the *AD* curve was constructed on the basis of the consumption, investment, demand for money and supply of money relationships. The *AD* curve will still be downward sloping from left to right. In Figure 5.8 when the price level is high (shown by point *a*), the income level is low. Lower price levels (points *b* and *c*) produce correspondingly higher income levels. The points of intersection for *P* and *Y* can therefore be transferred to Figure 5.9 to produce our familiar downward-sloping aggregate demand curve.

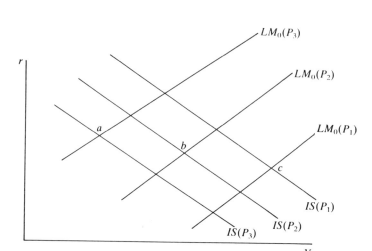

Figure 5.8 The effect of different price levels on the *IS* and *LM* curves

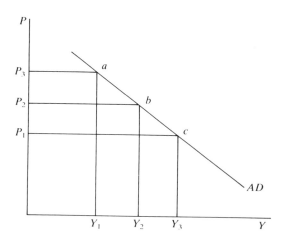

Figure 5.9 The aggregate demand curve

Since both the *LM* and the *IS* curves are uniquely related to the price level in the open economy framework, the relative size of the effect that a price change has on each of these curves will determine the shape of the *AD* curve (measured by the relative distance between each *IS* and *LM* curve). The slope of the *AD* curve will alter if the effect of a price change is greater for the *LM* curve than for the *IS* curve. It is likely for a developing country that the effect of a change in the price level on the *IS* curve will be small because the price elasticity of demand for exports is likely to be low. This means the *IS* curves shown in Figure 5.8 will be close together as the effect of a price change on exports and therefore on the *IS* curve is relatively small. In this case the *AD* curve would have a steeper slope than that shown in Figure 5.9.

With the *IS* and *LM* curves changing whenever the price level changes, the analysis can become cumbersome. If the student is unconvinced of this, add the effect of price changes to Figure 5.4 to see how the diagram quickly becomes crowded.

The analysis incorporating a variable price level and the external sector can be simplified by extending the four-quadrant analysis developed in Chapters 2 and 3. We begin by assuming that the foreign exchange rate, the rest of the world rate of interest and the rest of the world price level remain constant. A new *BP* curve can be constructed that shows equilibrium for various combinations of interest rate and price level. This is shown in Figure 5.10.

Any point on the curve represents a balance of payments equilibrium. Point *A* shows a disequilibrium situation with the price level at P_1 and the rate of interest at r_1. In this case either the price level is too high (it should be P_2) or the interest rate is too low (it should be r_2) to achieve balance of payments equilibrium. Position *A*, therefore, shows a balance of payments deficit. Indeed all points above the *BP* line show a balance of payments deficit, and all those below, a surplus.

Figure 5.10 does not show the actual rate of interest and price level. This can be determined by combining the analysis in Chapter 3 with the international sector. In this case we use the *AD* curve in conjunction with the relation between the rate of interest and the price level (the *RR* curve) that was specified from the *IS/LM* framework developed in Chapter 3. This is shown in Figure 5.11.

The *AD* curve shows the combinations of *P* and *Y* that give equilibrium in the goods and money sectors, and the *RR* curve

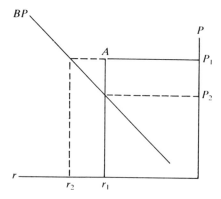

Figure 5.10 Derivation of *BP* curve holding the price level and the rate of interest in the rest of the world constant

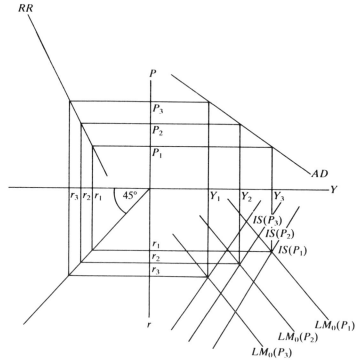

Figure 5.11 Derivation of *RR* curve showing relation between the price level and interest rates

shows the combinations of *P* and *r* that give equilibrium in the money sector. The actual price level and rate of interest are determined when the *AS* curve is added. This is shown in Figure 5.12 and is combined with the new formulated *BP* curve.

Figure 5.12 shows that the actual price level is P_0 and the rate of interest is r_0. The economy has a balance of payments deficit shown by the gap between the *RR* and *BP* curves (between points *a* and *b*). In this case there is internal equilibrium with an external disequilibrium. We examine whether or not this imbalance is stable later on in Chapter 8.

It will be useful to reinforce our understanding of the working of an open economy framework with a variable price level, by examining the variables held constant when the *BP* curve is constructed. It should be clear that the *BP* curve is constructed on the basis of its relationship to the price level and the rate of interest, even though the level of income is also an important component of the balance of payments. We have overcome this by assuming that the effect of a change in the level of income on the balance of payments works in the same direction as a change in the price level. This allows us to use the price axis in Figure 5.10 as a proxy for the effect that changes in income will have on the balance of payments. The student can check the logic of this assumption by examining the components of the import and export functions. An increase in the domestic price relative to the rest of the world price level and an increase in the level of domestic income will lead to a deterioration in the balance of payments and vice versa.

The *BP* curve has been constructed, therefore, from assumptions about the price level and its relationship to the income level. These assumptions were derived from a specific set of aggregate demand and supply curves. Since the upward-sloping *AS* curve depends on a particular fixed wage level, this must also be held constant for any given *BP* curve. A change in the fixed money wage will, therefore, lead to a shift in both the *AS* and the *BP* curves. An increase in the money wage will shift the *AS* curve to the left and the *BP* curve to the right. An increase in the money wage is shown in Figure 5.13 by shifting the *AS* curve leftwards. In this example the economy is initially in internal and external equilibrium. At each price level the equilibrium income level will be lower. At P_0 the equilibrium income level becomes Y_1 instead of Y_0. Each price level is therefore

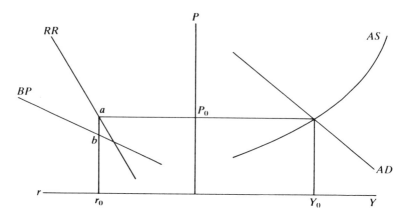

Figure 5.12 Internal equilibrium at below full employment with a balance of payments deficit

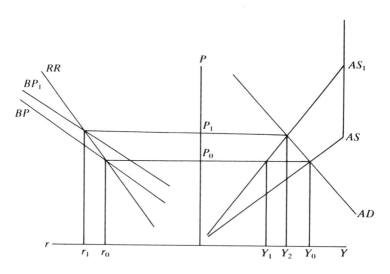

Figure 5.13 The effect of an increase in the money wage on the aggregate supply and balance of payments curves

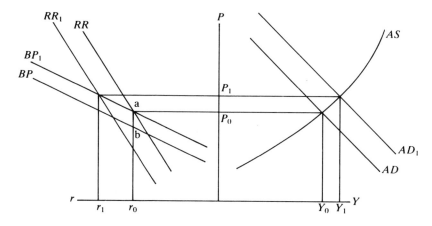

Figure 5.14 The effect of increasing tariffs on the balance of payments and domestic income

associated with a larger balance of trade since a lower income level implies a lower import level.

Since the actual price level increases to P_1 as a result of the change in the money wage, the rate of interest required to maintain a balance of payments equilibrium has to rise from r_0 to r_1. Of course, the effect this would have on the overall result depends on the other relationships specified and the subsequent actions taken. In the example in Figure 5.13 with a fixed exchange rate, the balance of payments equilibrium is maintained by the combined effect of a rise in interest rates and a fall in income offsetting the effect of a rise in the price level from P_0 to P_1.[2]

The *BP* curve will also be affected by changes in the exchange rate, the rest of the world rate of interest, the rest of the world price level and the level of taxation. An increase in the rest of the world price level, a reduction in the rest of the world interest rate, a fall in the exchange rate and an increase in the rate of taxation will shift the *BP* curve to the right.[3]

Finally, we can examine the effect a tariff change will have on the balance of payments. Tariffs in developing countries are used widely for government revenue purposes and as an instrument to control the balance of payments. In Figure 5.14 we examine the likely effects on the price level, income and balance of payments of an increase in tariffs. The relative price ratio in the import function can be modified to incorporate tariffs. Since these effectively raise the price paid by domestic residents for imports, they can be considered equivalent to raising the world price level.[4]

In our framework an increase in tariffs will raise the price of imports, which improves the balance of trade and encourages domestic producers to expand domestic production (substitution effect). In Figure 5.14 the AD curve shifts to the right and the RR curve to the left. The BP curve under these circumstances will also shift rightwards. If the initial situation is portrayed by internal equilibrium at below full employment with the price level at P_0, the income level at Y_0 and the domestic rate of interest at r_0 and by external disequilibrium shown by a balance of payments deficit ab, a rise in the tariff rate will increase P, r and Y and will reduce the balance of payments deficit. If, however, the increase in interest cost and in the price of imports (which have low price and income elasticities) raises domestic producer costs, the AS curve will also shift leftwards, and in turn will raise domestic prices and correspondingly worsen the balance of payments.

The effect that trade policy has on the BP curve through changes in the exchange rate and the various policy options available to deal with imbalance in the trade account are discussed in greater detail in Chapter 8. The appendix to this chapter provides a diagrammatic derivation of the BP curve.

Further reading

A review of the use of the diagrammatic approach to economic modelling can be found in Mundell (1962) and Johnson (1976) and in the textbooks of Perlman (1974) and Parkin and Bade (1982). A useful analysis of trade liberalisation which can be followed through using the framework developed in this and other chapters is given in Renshaw (1989). For a more advanced treatment see Williamson (1983).

Appendix: Derivation of *BP* curve

The balance of trade side is shown separately in Figures 5.15 and 5.16. Figure 5.15 shows the relationship between the price level and

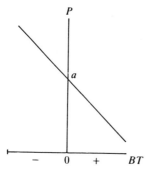

Figure 5.15   The balance of trade in relation to the price level

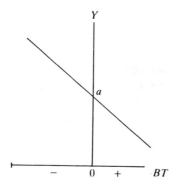

Figure 5.16   The balance of trade in relation to the level of income

the balance of trade. It shows the price level which will achieve a balance of trade position such that $BT = 0$. The curve is constructed with a downward slope from left to right, indicating that *ceteris paribus* an increase in the domestic price level worsens the balance of trade position, shown by points to the left of position *a*. This occurs since imports are increased and exports reduced as a result of an increase in the price level. Figure 5.16 shows the relation between the balance of trade and domestic income. This curve also slopes from left to right because *ceteris paribus* higher levels of domestic income, by increasing the demand for imports, worsen the balance of trade.

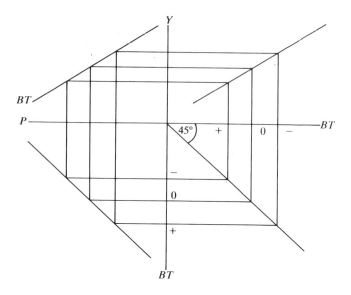

Figure 5.17 Derivation of the *BT* curve

Figures 5.15 and 5.16 can be inserted into a four quadrant diagram showing the combined effects of price and income on the balance of trade (Figure 5.17). In this case the price and income axes have been replotted to form the base of the four quadrant diagram. This is shown in the NW quadrant. The curve plotted in Figure 5.17 shows the equilibrium points ($BT = 0$) for the balance of trade where both determinants, Y and P, are considered.

The information given in the four quadrant diagrams is condensed and shown in Figure 5.18. In this diagram the price level is shown on the vertical axis and income is shown in a similar manner to the demand for money function described in Chapter 2. This time, however, lower levels of income are shown by the higher curves, such that $Y_4 > Y_3 > Y_2 > Y_1$.

The price level P_1 shows that at income Y_4 the balance of trade position is zero. At a higher price level, say P_2, with income held constant at Y_4, the balance of trade deteriorates. Similarly, at successively lower income levels, for example as we move from Y_4 to Y_3, with the price level held constant at P_1, the balance of trade

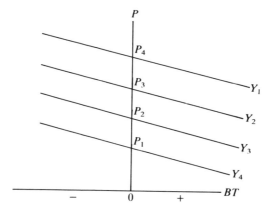

Figure 5.18 Balance of trade with different price and income levels

improves. Figure 5.18 effectively captures the relationships shown in Figures 5.15 and 5.16.

We now turn to the capital account of the balance of payments. Figure 5.19 shows that, if we hold the rest of the world interest rate constant (r_w), there will be some interest rate that gives a net capital flow of zero. This is shown by r_0. Similarly, with r_w held constant, an interest rate higher than r_0 will lead to a net capital inflow.

We saw from Figure 5.18 the combination of income and price level that provided a balance of trade equal to zero. This means that the value of imports is equal to the value of exports. Since a higher price level or a higher income leads to a balance of trade deficit, there must be a rate of interest which produces a net capital inflow sufficient to offset this deficit. This relation is hypothesised in Figure 5.20, which gives the relationship between the price level and the balance of trade and between the rate of interest and the capital balance.

It is a simple matter to trace the combinations of P and r required for balance of payments equilibrium. These are shown in the NW quadrant depicted by points a, b and c and labelled *BP*. In effect this curve shows combinations of r, P and Y which bring about balance of payments equilibrium. This is the case because it can be assumed that changes in P have the same directional effect on the balance of payments as changes in Y.

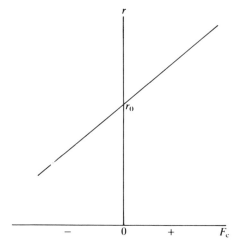

Figure 5.19   Net capital inflows

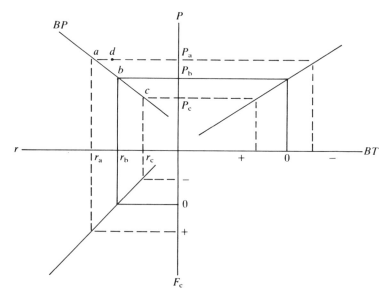

Figure 5.20   Derivation of the *BP* curve

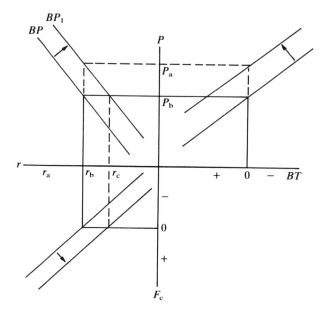

Figure 5.21 The effect of a shift in the *BP* curve

Point *b* in the NW quadrant shows that r_b and P_b produce a balance in both the trade and capital accounts. Point *a* shows that the balance of trade deficit, caused by a price level of P_a, is exactly offset by the capital account surplus produced by r_a. A balance of trade surplus is similarly offset by an interest rate of r_c.

It can be seen that point *d* represents a balance of payments disequilibrium. At point *d* the price level of P_a is too high to achieve $BP = 0$ or the interest rate of r_b is too low.

The *BP* curve shifts to the left or right when the variables held constant along its length change. A change in one of these variables (tax rate, wage rate, exchange rate, etc.) alters the combination of price level and rate of interest needed to maintain balance of payments equilibrium.

Figure 5.21 shows a rightward shift of the *BP* curve. Balance of payments equilibrium is now achieved by a combination of r_b and P_a. In this case the curve in the NE quadrant shifts to the left. For a given rate of interest each price level is associated with an improvement in the balance of trade. Similarly, for a given price level a lower rate of interest is required to achieve $BP = 0$. In this case at P_b a rate of interest of r_c achieves equilibrium and the curve in the SW quadrant shifts rightwards. Alternatively, both curves in the NE and SW quadrants can shift to produce BP_1. In this case the new curves would lie between those shown.

Notes

1. A rise in the rate of interest in the rest of the world (r_w) will worsen the balance of payments. Check that you understand why the BP curve shifts to the left in this situation by referring to Figures 5.1 and 5.2.
2. If the BP curve shifts further than shown in Figure 5.13, there will be a balance of payments surplus. In this case if no sterilisation takes place, the AD and RR curves will shift to restore internal and external equilibrium. This is discussed in Chapters 7 and 8.
3. These variables are held constant along a particular BP curve. It will be useful to work out why a change in the level of taxation leads to a shift in the BP curve while a change in government expenditure does not.
4. Similarly, an export subsidy will lower the domestic price to foreign buyers. Both the tariff and the subsidy will enter the budget constraint discussion in Chapter 7, where the subsidy becomes part of government expenditure and the tariff receipts are part of government revenue.

6

Policy instruments and targets

We have now seen that macroeconomic policy aims to achieve stabilisation of the main economic variables – real output, balance of payments and price level. The variables represent the policy makers' target variables. To achieve their stabilisation objectives, the policy makers have a variety of policy instruments at their disposal which can be used to bring about the desired changes in the target variables. The problem is to know which instruments to use to achieve stabilisation in each of the target variables.

6.1 Policy and targets

A partial solution to this problem is provided by the general rule that there must be at least as many instruments as targets if all targets are to be attained. This is known as 'the theory of economic policy'. But which instruments do we use? It has been proposed that the rule described above should be complemented by what is called 'the principle of effective market classification', which concerns the pairing of targets and instruments. This is based on the argument that instruments should be 'assigned' to the target on which they have most influence. In other words, one policy instrument is used to pursue one target.

The assignment approach to the choice of policy instruments can be illustrated using Figure 6.1. We assume that there are two targets – balance of payments equilibrium and real output equilibrium

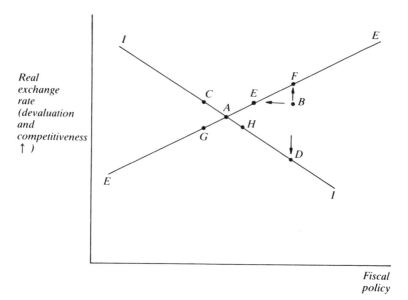

Figure 6.1 Internal and external equilibrium for various combinations of fiscal policy and real exchange rates

(what we described earlier as internal and external equilibrium). There are two policy instruments, fiscal policy and the exchange rate. Fiscal policy, as we have seen, can be used to raise aggregate output, but at the expense of worsening the balance of payments by raising import demand. Devaluation of the exchange rate will improve international competitiveness and the balance of payments, but at the same time will increase the level of aggregate demand. Figure 6.1 shows internal and external equilibrium curves, for various combinations of fiscal policy and the (real) exchange rate. The downward slope of the *II* curve shows that, for output to be kept at the target equilibrium level, a more expansive fiscal policy must be offset by an exchange rate change (revaluation). Points above *II* represent income levels that exceed the target level; by similar argument, points to the left of and below *II* represent combinations of the exchange rate and fiscal policy that sustain a below-target income level. The *EE* curve shows combinations of the two policy instruments that produce the target balance of payments equilibrium. Points above *EE* represent a surplus balance of payments situation; points to the right and below, a deficit. Point *A* represents internal and external equilibrium. Suppose that initially the economy is at *B*, with a balance of payments deficit and excess output. If fiscal policy alone is used, internal equilibrium will be reached at *C*, but there will be a balance of payments surplus. If the exchange rate alone is altered, we could achieve internal balance at *D*, but the balance of payments would be in deficit. By similar reasoning, external equilibrium could be achieved by shifting from *B* to *E* or *F*, but in both cases there is internal disequilibrium. However, if both fiscal policy and exchange rate policy are used, the economy can achieve both targets, by moving from *B* to *A*.

Suppose we assign one instrument to each policy-making authority; can internal and external balance be reached if the policy makers act independently and without co-operation? Assume fiscal policy is assigned to the output target and the exchange rate to the balance of payments target. If we begin again at *B*, the authority responsible for output management (the 'Treasury' or 'Ministry of Finance') will cut expenditure and move the economy to *C*. The Central Bank does not intervene at this stage, since the reduction in output level is improving the balance of payments. But when the economy reaches internal equilibrium at *C* there is a surplus in the balance of payments and the Central Bank will revalue the exchange rate, shifting to point *G*. The Treasury responds to the below-target level of income by adopting an expansionary fiscal policy, moving the economy to *H*. The process continues, with the economy converging to internal and external equilibrium at *A*. So far so good. Policy assignment appears to work.

But suppose we start with an alternative assignment, linking the exchange rate to internal balance and fiscal policy to external balance. The adjustment process in this case is shown in Figure 6.2.

We begin again at *B*, where there is a balance of payments deficit and excess output. The Treasury is now responsible for external balance and therefore cuts aggregate expenditure, moving the economy to *C*. The Central Bank, which is now responsible for internal balance, revalues the exchange rate and shifts to *D*. At *D* the balance of payments is still in deficit and the Treasury implements a further cut in expenditure, shifting the economy to *E*. The process continues, with the economy diverging from, rather than converging towards, the internal and external equilibrium point *A*.

What we see, therefore, is that assigning a target to a particular instrument can work, but the assignment needs to be correct. It is argued that the correct assignment is when instruments are attached to the target on which they have relatively greater influence.

The underlying theme of this book is that there is no single analytical framework or model appropriate for tackling the problems of macro instability in developing countries. The institutional and structural characteristics of each national economy differ, and these differences will influence the impact that a given policy measure has on the target variables. The choice of policy instruments and their assignment to particular policy targets will depend, therefore, on our view of how a particular economy functions.

A second qualification to the assignment solution to the choice of policy instruments is that in practice policy measures are, quite correctly, not taken in isolation from each other. Rather than the unrealistic process of sequential policy adjustment assumed in Figures 6.1 and 6.2, policy makers will be attempting to co-ordinate their decisions, aiming to achieve internal and external equilibrium simultaneously. Policy making is therefore much more complicated than the simple assignment analysis suggests.

Nevertheless, the assignment principle does provide a useful way of simplifying the economic policy-making process, and it has been used widely in developing the basic theory of macroeconomic policy. We follow the same approach in the next three chapters, where our three main target variables are related to single policy instruments. Aggregate expenditure policy is assigned to the real output level; exchange rate policy to the balance of payments; and wages policy to inflation. The two qualifications made to the assignment approach will, however, be allowed for in the analysis. In each chapter where a single target is discussed (Chapters 7, 8 and 9), we consider how different structural characteristics of the economy will influence the impact of a given policy instrument, and will determine the choice of instrument to be assigned to the target variable. In the final chapter we will give an integrated analysis of stabilisation policy which will illustrate how a range of policy instruments can be used simultaneously to achieve overall equilibrium in the economy.

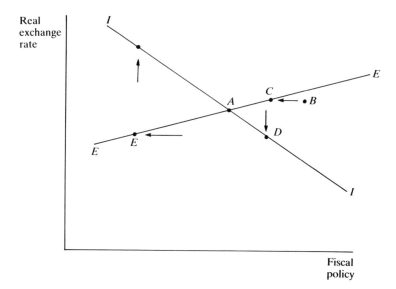

Figure 6.2 Real exchange rate and fiscal policy

Besides the assignment problem which concerns the type of instrument to use to change specified target variables, policy makers are faced with the added problem of conducting policy under conditions of uncertainty. The analysis in this book assumes that the underlying structure of the economic framework or model is known to the policy makers, and that they design and implement policy with a full knowledge of the positions of the curves and schedules. In reality, of course, the functions are subject to stochastic disturbances. We allow for this by changing the positions and slopes of the various curves, so that they can be assumed to be affected by variations, but the underlying form of the model is unchanged.

The existence of stochastic variations in the macro system has led to the use of intermediate variables in the formulation of economic policy. Intermediate variables and objectives occupy a position between the policy instruments and the final target variables. If information about the behaviour of the intermediate variable is more quickly available than data about the final objective, and if the

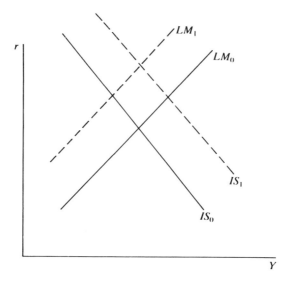

Figure 6.3 Policy response to real sector shocks

intermediate target has a stable relationship with the final objective, then the use of the intermediate variable may enable the policy maker to respond more rapidly to the unanticipated shock to the economy.

Suppose that the policy makers know from past experience that the system is subject to periodic real sector shocks, e.g. in the consumption or investment function. This causes the *IS* curve to shift from IS_0 to IS_1 in Figure 6.3. In the short run, the authorities will not have direct information on the behaviour of the output level which is the target variable. They will, however, observe an immediate increase in the rate of interest and, since they know that the disturbance occurred in the real side of the economy, they can immediately deduce that the correct policy response will be to shift the *LM* curve to the left from LM_0 to LM_1 by reducing the money stock.

In this case, then, the rapidly available information on the rate of interest allows the authorities to use the money supply as an intermediate policy instrument, thereby reducing the size of the output fluctuations resulting from the initial disturbance.

6.2 Dynamic adjustment

Our examination of the economy has proceeded through comparative statics. This approach involves moving from one equilibrium point to another, comparing the old with the new. It is well known that the final impact of a change in an economic variable on the economy cannot be determined without an explicit examination of the underlying dynamic process of adjustment. When a policy variable is changed, a dynamic analysis is required to see whether a new equilibrium is actually achieved. Policy makers are also interested in knowing how long it takes for the adjustment process to work and what path it takes to reach a new equilibrium position. The length of time and the path taken to reach a new equilibrium position are important because actions that take a long time to achieve their results, and especially those that oscillate to a new equilibrium, may affect subsequent policy changes.

We have not been able to analyse the difficult dynamic process in this text. There are, however, four basic types of time and path that reflect the movement of the economy over time from the old equilibrium to the new equilibrium. These are a smooth movement, a fluctuating movement, an initially explosive movement whose oscillations become larger and larger moving away from equilibrium, and finally an explosive path that moves directly away from equilibrium. The first two types move from one equilibrium to another, and the smooth type best represents the process underlying much of the comparative static analysis in this text.

Analysis of the dynamic process, however, reveals important points about the comparative static approach we have adopted. It clearly takes time to move from one equilibrium position to another, and implicit in the analysis in this book are the assumptions that the economy actually achieves a new equilibrium and that during this adjustment the economy has the time required to complete the process for the problem under consideration.

We can relate dynamic analysis to the models developed in this book by considering them in two parts. First, in Chapter 2 we developed a simple demand-side model where in disequilibrium producers reacted to excess demand for goods and services by increasing their output. Through the multiplier process, the economy moved to a new equilibrium position since the marginal propensity to consume was less than one. We were not able to examine the intensity of the producers' reaction to the size of excess demand. How do producers respond to the imbalance between demand and supply that they are expected to reduce? Producers being individuals may react differently to the situation, some increasing output slowly to avoid risk, others even overreacting. Producers' reaction to the supply and demand imbalance will determine to what extent the system moves smoothly or oscillates, perhaps *en route* overshooting, towards equilibrium.

Second, in terms of the *IS/LM* framework developed in Chapter 2, there are two sectors, the goods and the money sectors, that could be in disequilibrium. The two assumptions made regarding the working of the economy in a disequilibrium situation are that producers respond to excess demand and that the rate of interest adjusts to remove disequilibrium in the money sector. If the monetary sector is efficient and institutions are well developed, adjustment will be faster.

The direction and the intensity of an economy's response to a disequilibrium are not the only factors affecting the path to equilibrium. This is also affected by the behavioural relationships specified. If, for example, the *LM* curve slopes steeply as a result of an interest-inelastic demand for money function, and the *IS* curve is more horizontal as the demand for investment is highly responsive to changes in the interest rate, then an increase in the supply of money will cause a small fall in the rate of interest. This adjustment path would not be shown in the *IS* and *LM* diagrams in this book. Adjustment from an old equilibrium to a new equilibrium is shown as a one-shot shift in a particular curve and a movement along the other. The dynamic adjustment path in the above example is likely to oscillate because an increase in the money supply would cause a large fall in the interest rate due to the interest inelasticity of the demand for money. This in turn would cause a large rise in investment because investment demand is highly interest elastic.

As a concluding point it is important to recognise that, whatever the set of behavioural relationships specified for the economy, the adjustment path by which the economy changes may be considerably more complex than those used in this text.

Further reading

Killick (1981, chs. 1–3) gives an introductory discussion of policy instruments and targets in the context of developing countries. A more formal treatment of the macroeconomic policy design issues is presented in Levacic (1987) and Stevenson, Muscatelli and Gregory (1988, ch. 9).

7

Demand management policy

In this chapter we examine the main components of demand management, fiscal and monetary policy. In the first part of the chapter we separate the two types of policy and compare their separate effects on real income. Following this we bring the analysis of monetary and fiscal policy together through the budget constraint. In the latter part of the chapter we extend the previous analysis, which has been for the most part confined to the closed economy, to consider the implications of monetary and fiscal policy for the open developing economy. This subject is again taken up in relation to the exchange rate in Chapters 8 and 10.

7.1 Fiscal and monetary policy

The aim of fiscal policy is the management of the government budget, which consists of different types of expenditure and revenue. Government expenditure is divided into current (or recurrent) expenditure, consisting of consumption, subsidies and salaries and wages for the public sector, and capital expenditure (public sector fixed investment). Government revenue is derived from taxes on income and domestic goods, and taxes on trade (import duties or tariffs and export taxes). In developing countries, income taxes seldom represent the most important source of government revenue. Monetary policy is used by government to regulate the money supply and the supply of credit, the structure of credit and the level and structure of interest rates, in order to achieve its desired economic objectives.

In many developing countries, monetary policy has played a less prominent role than fiscal policy owing to the lack of development in the banking and financial infrastructure, and consequently the role of financial intermediation in facilitating borrowing and lending has been limited. In this situation it is up to fiscal policy to capture private savings and translate them into investment, largely through government capital expenditure programmes. While a proportion of new investment is financed through taxation, as we shall see in the discussion of the budget constraint, a significant amount of public sector investment is financed through increases in the supply of money. In the next sections we examine the characteristics of each type of policy. In order to separate clearly the effects of each type of policy, it is necessary to make a number of restrictive assumptions.

7.2 Fiscal policy

Pure fiscal policy can be defined as a budgetary change which leaves the nominal money supply unchanged. In this case the change in fiscal policy is represented by a shift in the *IS* curve and a movement along a specific *LM* curve. This can be accomplished by assuming that increased government expenditure is financed by issuing government bonds so that the government borrows from the private sector. The quantity of money or reserve assets available to the economy does not change. We examine the alternative ways in which the government can finance its expenditure when we consider the budget constraint later in this chapter. A given change in government expenditure, then, shifts the *IS* curve by the change in government expenditure times the multiplier. This is given by

$$\Delta Y = \Delta G \frac{1}{1 - b(1 - t)} \tag{7.1}$$

t is the tax rate related to income and *b* is the marginal propensity to consume.

The full effect of a change in government expenditure on real income in the *IS/LM* framework is equal to the above multiplier

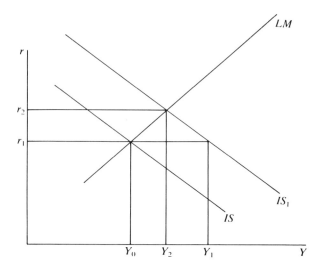

Figure 7.1   An increase in government expenditure

effect less the effect the change in expenditure has on the rate of interest. The change in the rate of interest curtails part of the change in desired expenditure. Figure 7.1 shows that the full multiplier effect given by equation (7.1) is moderated by the effect the change in the interest rate has on desired expenditure. It can be seen that an increase in government expenditure shifts the *IS* curve from *IS* to IS_1. The full multiplier effect on income is shown by Y_0Y_1. Since the increase in government expenditure causes disequilibrium in the money market which leads to a rise in the rate of interest, the equilibrium level of real income finally attained is Y_2 not Y_1.

This effect, referred to as 'crowding out', will be larger if an increase in expenditure also leads to an increase in the price level. This effect can be illustrated using a portion of the four quadrant analysis developed earlier.

Figure 7.2 shows that an increase in government expenditure shifts the *AD* curve from position *a* to *b* if the full multiplier effect operates. But the change in the rate of interest following the increase in government expenditure restricts the movement of the *AD* curve to position *c* (i.e. *AD* to AD_1). The effectiveness of a change in government expenditure on the level of real income is

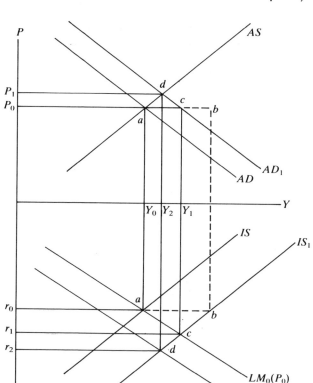

Figure 7.2 The interest rate and price level effect on the multiplier

further restricted by the increase in the price level. This effect is represented by a movement along AD_1 from point c to d. This movement is shown by the leftward shift in the LM curve from $LM_0(P_0)$ to $LM_0(P_1)$ in the lower section of the diagram. The LM curve shifts because the real money supply is reduced by the increase in the price level. The final position attained following an increase in government expenditure, accounting for changes in both the interest rate and the price level, is d. At this point, income is Y_2 and the price level is P_1.

So far we have assumed that taxation and the nominal money

supply have been held constant while an increase in government expenditure has been financed by an increase in the supply of government bonds to the private sector. This enabled us to look at the effects of government expenditure on real income. Under this assumption the ultimate effect on real income was equal to the government expenditure multiplier less the rate of interest and price effects on expenditure.

We can now compare the effect of an increase in government expenditure with a reduction in the level of taxation. A change in taxes is not in itself a change in aggregate demand. A change in taxes works through its effect on consumption behaviour. In Chapter 2 we showed that consumption is related to disposable income and, since taxation affects the relationship between total income and disposable income, then a change in taxation will eventually lead to a change in consumption. The effect on real income is then given by

$$\Delta Y = -b\Delta t_0 \frac{1}{1 - b(1 - t)} \tag{7.2}$$

Since a change in taxes (Δt_0) changes consumption by $-b\Delta t_0$, equation (7.2) shows the shift in the *IS* curve resulting from a given change in taxes. It can be seen by comparing this with equation (7.1) that equal changes in government expenditure and taxes are non-neutral in their effect on aggregate demand. A proportional increase in both gives a net expansionary effect on the level of real output.

7.3   Monetary policy

The aim of monetary policy in developing countries is twofold. In the first instance, monetary policy can be viewed as influencing aggregate demand through the regulation of interest rates, credit availability and credit allocation. This role refers to stabilisation. Within stabilisation policy there is disagreement over the extent to which government ought to intervene to control monetary instruments and the extent to which the market mechanism should determine the direction in which variables move. Monetary policy also has a role in promoting growth. Its primary task is to transfer resources from areas where resources are in surplus supply to those where they are in greater demand for investment purposes. In general the motivation for this reallocation is to improve the profitability of investment. In this book we concentrate on the role of monetary policy in stabilisation, which is essentially aimed at controlling inflation. Nevertheless, our theoretical understanding of how money and monetary policy affect the growth process is increasing, and policy makers will need to consider the longer-run consequences of shorter-term policies.

The principal way in which monetary policy is implemented is through changes in the money supply. As shown in Chapter 2, a change in the supply of money shifts the *LM* curve, either to the right or to the left. The change in income as a result of a change in the quantity of money occurs through portfolio adjustment. The change in the money stock causes an imbalance between the demand for and supply of money, which in turn leads to a change in the rate of interest. The rate of interest acts as a mechanism for achieving equilibrium. This process is illustrated in Figure 7.3. The money supply is increased from LM_0 to LM_1. At interest rate r_0 there is excess supply of money, and individuals will attempt to reduce their money balances by buying bonds. This will raise the price of bonds in the bond market and lower the rate of interest until equilibrium is achieved at r_1.

This straightforward result is obtained when the portfolio concerns a choice between two assets, bonds and money. In reality, the choice is likely to be much wider, in which case the effect on the rate of interest of creating an imbalance through changing the money supply is less clear. While rates of return on the total range of alternative assets are likely to change in the same direction, the effect on the interest rate will be less specific. There may also be a more direct effect on income than through the effect on investment of changing interest rates. This occurs where the excess in the supply of money is channelled into extra expenditure. This happens because the increase in the supply of money represents an increase in wealth. In this case both the *IS* and *LM* curves will shift to the right when the money supply is increased, with the result that the interest rate may remain unchanged. This situation is indicated by the intersection of IS_1 and LM_1 in Figure 7.3.

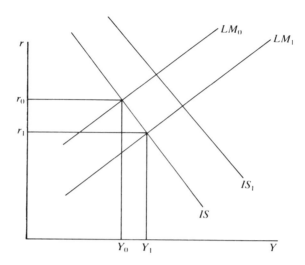

Figure 7.3 Effect of a change in the money supply on the interest rate and income level

So far we have examined how a change in the supply of money affects the level of real income either through portfolio adjustment, where the interest rate is an instrumental variable affecting the level of investment (seen as a shift in the *LM* curve and a movement along the *IS* curve) and reducing the imbalance between the supply and demand for money; or through the direct effect of a change in the quantity of money on consumption expenditure (a shift in the *LM* and *IS* curves). It is now necessary to turn our attention to the ways in which the money supply may be changed.

7.4 Monetary instruments

We saw in Chapter 4 that a change in the money supply occurs when there is a change in the monetary base or high-powered money. Changes in the monetary base can be seen through the operation of the following monetary instruments. If we ignore for the moment the effect the balance of payments has on the money base, then the Central Bank can influence the money supply through its control of the quantity of its credit made available to the banking sector and the government, its control over the reserve requirements, and its ability to persuade banks to change their behaviour.

Central Bank credit can be changed directly throuɡn its *refinancing* facilities which apply directly to banks or other eligible borrowers. Obviously the use of this facility in monetary policy will vary according to who is the borrower and the rules and regulations established in a particular country. The Central Bank might establish automatic or discretionary lines of credit to eligible borrowers, i.e. banks, although the Central Bank can also regulate borrowing of this type with the interest rate, known as the base rate or discount rate. In the case of private commercial banks, the Central Bank, acting in its capacity as banker to the banking system, holds their deposits. Sometimes these deposits also form part of the banks' cash reserves. Since the private banks will be required to repay deposits in cash on demand, if they run short of cash reserves these can be borrowed from the Central Bank at the discount rate. In general the use of this type of credit facility is usually limited to discounting high-quality assets or lending on the basis of high-quality collateral, which is a feature that will limit the supply of this form of credit in developing countries.

The base rate or bank rate is then used to determine the direction of monetary policy by indicating whether it is expansionary or contractionary, although it should be borne in mind that it is not just the level of the bank rate which determines whether or not monetary policy is expansionary or contractionary, but also the spread of rates between the bank or discount rate and the rates at which the commercial banks can borrow from other sources. The Central Bank can therefore attempt to control credit to the commercial banks by raising or lowering the bank rate. If the Central Bank wants to restrict the money supply, it can raise the base rate to a level which makes it unattractive for the banks to borrow from it. This instrument is effective, then, only to the extent that banks borrow from the Central Bank.

Another way in which Central Bank credit (base money) can be made available (reduced) is through the purchase (sale) of government bonds in secondary markets rather than directly with banks. The use of this instrument, known as *open market operations*, to change the money base is dependent on the depth of the asset or bond market and its quality. The precise way in which open market operations lead to a change in the money supply was explained in Chapter 4. The market has to be of a sufficient size that the Central Bank's dealings do not disrupt or totally control the market. In many developing countries the secondary market for assets is poorly developed, ruling out the effective use of open market operations as a mechanism for changing the money supply.

Since the Central Bank is the government's bank, the government can directly finance its budgetary deficit by borrowing from the Central Bank. This is common practice in developing countries where the use of open market operations is limited. In situations where the bond market is poorly developed and government borrowing directly from individuals in the private sector is very limited, the government may sell bonds to the commercial banks. In this way the government indirectly taps the private savings of individuals, not through their direct purchase of bonds but through their savings deposits held in banks. In some cases the government attempts to force banks to hold the government's debt instruments, but in cases where the private banks are unwilling to purchase all the bonds issued, the Central Bank itself underwrites the issue. In this case the government is effectively borrowing from the Central Bank.

The monetary authority or Central Bank can influence the size of the money supply by regulating the *reserve requirements* of the commercial banks. As seen in Chapter 4, the reserve requirement has a direct effect on the size of the money multiplier for a given money base. The reserve requirement is an important instrument of monetary control in developing countries, although the accuracy with which the Central Bank can control the money supply through manipulating reserve requirements depends also on the reserve policy of the commercial banks. If the banks, as part of their own policy, hold reserves beyond those legally stipulated (a cautious reserve policy) then a given change in the legal reserve ratio will be less effective in changing the amount of credit available. Banks can also attempt to evade the legally applied reserve requirements, in which case the Central Bank may impose the payment of interest on required reserves.

Credit ceilings can also be imposed on the banks which will restrict their creation of credit from deposits. With a credit ceiling imposed by the Central Bank, banks are forced to hold idle reserves as deposits are made. Once a credit ceiling is reached, the money supply is constrained from further expansion. However, for credit ceilings to be effective they must work to prevent the expansion of lending not only in domestic but also in foreign markets. If the credit ceiling is applied only to the domestic market, banks can lend any excess deposits abroad. In the case of developing countries, additional controls have often prevented this happening.

Finally, *interest rate* policy has played an important role in the range of monetary instruments used in developing countries. Most often it has been used to influence saving and investment behaviour. Policy makers in developing countries have faced two sets of problems in dealing with interest rates. The first relates to the level at which overall rates should be established. Should they be high or low? One argument stresses that the interest rate reflects the price of capital and that, since capital is relatively scarce in developing countries, the interest rate ought to be high. A high interest rate will therefore encourage domestic saving. A different view emphasises that interest rates represent the cost of investment and as such should be kept low to encourage investment.

The second problem relates to the use of the interest rate as a monetary tool. While it might be desirable to lower interest rates to stimulate investment, this is usually achieved by increasing the quantity of money, which might then be inflationary. Monetary expansion may then in turn lead to a more restrictive monetary policy which raises interest rates. The use of interest rates as a monetary tool will be constrained by their use in longer-term development policy.

Of course, all the policy instruments described will work differently depending on each country's institutional development and degree of integration between various financial markets. If financial markets are less developed and fragmented, some types of policy instrument will be excluded altogether. At the same time, some instruments reinforce the working of others. Open market operations might, for example, be used to supplement the effects of a discount rate change if the Central Bank felt discount rate changes would not affect aggregate demand sufficiently.

Although these instruments will be used to varying degrees in developing countries depending on the state of financial markets and institutional development, in less sophisticated markets the reserve ratio is likely to have a greater importance than discount rates and open market operations for changing the money supply.

This is particularly the case for banking systems that have excess liquidity: when banks are not fully loaned up, the Central Bank's ability to change other rates by changing the bank or discount rate is weakened because these instruments are designed to work on the margin.

7.5 Budget constraint

By assuming in the preceding sections that a government can increase its expenditure by bond issues to the private sector we have separated fiscal and monetary policy. Indeed, up until this point we have considered changes in the money supply, the level of taxation and government expenditure separately. In changing the level of any one of these variables we have assumed that the others remained constant. It is now time to combine them by introducing the so-called budget constraint. In a closed economy, a government can finance its expenditure by changing the money supply, raising taxation and issuing bonds.

If we assume that the budget is initially balanced by government expenditure being equal to tax revenue, then the constraint can be represented by the following set of equations:

$$\Delta G = \Delta C_u + \bar{T} + \bar{B}_d$$

or

$$\Delta G = \bar{C}_u + \Delta T + \bar{B}_d$$

or

$$\Delta G = \bar{C}_u + \bar{T} + \Delta B_d$$

where G represents government expenditure,
C_u is the quantity of currency,
T is the level of tax revenue,
B_d is the amount of government bonds.

Of course, ΔG can also take place by a combination of changes in the other variables, but in any event, at least one must change to finance a change in government expenditure.

We are now in a position to examine the interrelationship between the different types of policy by looking at their effects on the level of real income and the rate of interest. To simplify the

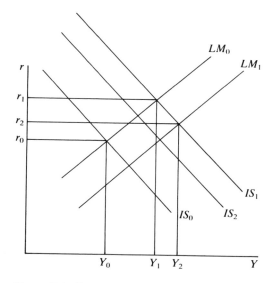

Figure 7.4 Impact of different ways of financing government
expenditure

comparison we assume that the price level is constant. Assuming an
initially balanced budget (where $G = T$), an increase in government expenditure will shift the *IS* curve to the right. The extent of
the shift in the *IS* curve, and whether or not the *LM* curve also
shifts, will depend on the way in which the increased expenditure is
financed.

If government expenditure is financed by issuing bonds, in Figure
7.4 the *IS* curve shifts from IS_0 to IS_1 and real output rises from Y_0 to
Y_1 and the rate of interest from r_0 to r_1. When expenditure is
financed by increasing the quantity of money (printing money) the
LM curve also shifts and in this case the rate of interest changes to r_2
and the income level to Y_2. Finally, if the change in government
expenditure is financed by an increase in taxation, the *IS* curve shifts
to IS_2, which lies to the left of IS_1. This reflects the differential
impact of a tax change on expenditure. In the case of both bond- and
tax-financed expenditure, the *LM* curve does not shift since the
nominal money supply remains unchanged.

The budget constraint is just as relevant to monetary policy as it is
to fiscal policy. This can be seen clearly by referring to a reduction in
the money supply which may be used in an attempt to control

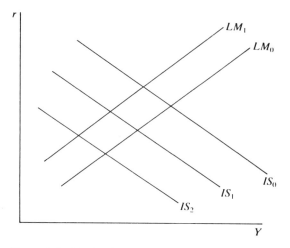

Figure 7.5   Reduction in the money supply with a budgetary constraint

inflation. (The efficacy of this type of policy for combating inflationary pressures is examined in greater detail in Chapter 9.) The government can reduce the money supply by selling bonds and holding expenditure and taxation constant, by increasing the level of taxes and holding expenditure constant, and by decreasing expenditure and holding taxes constant.[1] These are illustrated in Figure 7.5.

In the first case the LM curve moves from LM_0 to LM_1 along the IS curve IS_0. In the second case the LM shifts to LM_1 while the IS curve moves leftwards from IS_0 to IS_1 as the change in taxation reduces aggregate demand. In the final case the LM curve shifts to LM_1, but this time the leftward shift in the IS curve extends to IS_2 since the multiplier for a change in expenditure is larger than that for taxation. In the latter two cases there will be a budget surplus, the proceeds of which are withheld by the government to cause the fall in the money supply.

7.6   Budget deficit

The government will be deficit financing its budget when there is an imbalance between its revenue (collected through taxation and duties, and profits and dividends from public enterprises) and government expenditure (which includes subsidies). In terms of the budget constraint, therefore, the budget deficit can be financed by changing the quantity of money and/or the amount of bonds. In the case of an open economy framework, as will be seen in Chapter 8, this may be expanded to include foreign borrowing.

We can now compare the effect on the price level, the interest rate and the level of output of these two ways of financing the budget deficit. In Figure 7.6 the initial situation is given by P_0, r_0 and Y_0, which result from a balanced budget. An increase in government expenditure financed by selling bonds is shown by the shift in

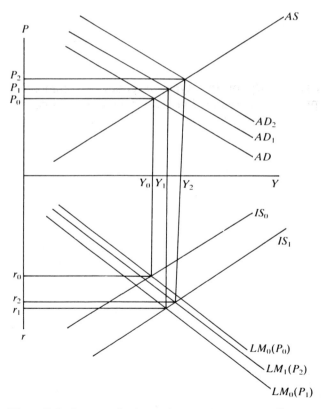

Figure 7.6 Impact of a change in government expenditure on the *IS*, *LM* and *AD* curves

the IS curve from IS_0 to IS_1 and the corresponding movement along the LM curve $LM_0(P_0)$. The LM curve will eventually shift in this case not because the nominal money supply has changed, but because there has been a change in the real supply of money as a result of the change in the price level. The LM curve shifts to $LM_0(P_1)$ and equilibrium is achieved at P_1, r_1 and Y_1.

In the case of an increase in government expenditure that is financed by changing the quantity of money, the IS curve shifts to IS_1 but the LM curve shifts to $LM_1(P_2)$, incorporating the effects of a change in the nominal quantity of money and in the real supply of money as the price level goes to P_2. The final equilibrium is then attained at P_2, r_2 and Y_2.

In the case of increased expenditure that is financed by changing the quantity of money there is also a need to examine the short- and long-run equilibrium. When a change in government expenditure shifts the IS curve and is financed by a change in the money stock, the LM curve does not just move from LM_0 to LM_1, but continues to shift as long as the budget deficit continues. This is because the fiscal deficit underlying the IS_1 curve in our example represents a flow magnitude, while the financial assets used to finance a budget deficit are a stock. We are, therefore, in a situation where the effect on the IS curve is a once and for all change, whereas the LM curve is continually shifting as long as the deficit persists.

Several other changes may occur through wealth effects. These can operate on both the IS and LM curves. A wealth effect may, for example, shift the LM curve because the increase in the quantity of money shown in Figure 7.6 causes an increase in the wealth stock, which leads to an increase in the demand for money. This will shift the LM curve leftwards in the opposite direction to the effect that an increase in the money supply has on the LM curve. Wealth effects may also act on the IS curve because they lead to a change in the level of consumption. In this case an increase in wealth leads to an increase in consumption, shifting the IS curve to the right.[2]

The combined effects of wealth working through the IS and LM curves as a result of an increase in government expenditure could take the form shown in Figure 7.7. The arrows indicate the direction for each type of change. If we assume that the price level is constant, the initial shift in government expenditure is shown by (1). The change in the quantity of money to finance the change in government expenditure is shown by (2). The IS shifts further as a result of

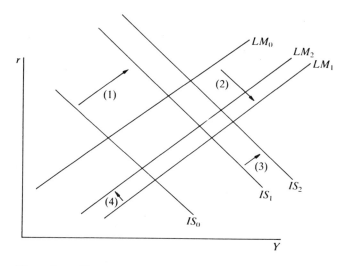

Figure 7.7   The wealth effects of an increase in government expenditure

the induced effect through wealth on consumption shown by (3), and the *LM* shifts in the opposite direction (4) as an increase in the quantity of money increases the stock of wealth which leads to an increase in demand for money.

In practice most governments will use a combination of bonds and money to finance their expenditure. Figure 7.6 indicated that financing the budget deficit through changes in the money stock, although expansionary, could be inflationary. In contrast, bond-financed expenditure which does not affect the quantity of money is likely to be less inflationary.

7.7   Crowding out

We are now in a position to summarise what we know about crowding out which concerns the efficacy of fiscal policy in stimulating aggregate demand. It refers to the way in which private sector spending is crowded out by changes in public expenditure. Indirect crowding out of private expenditure occurs by the rate of interest and price level effects of government expenditure. These effects were shown to curtail the full multiplier effect of government expenditure. In Figure 7.2 an increase in government expenditure financed by issuing bonds pushed up the interest rate, which eventually permitted the level of income to rise. Even though private sector investment was discouraged by a higher rate of interest, the impact of government expenditure on income was enough to outweigh this effect. Similarly, the increase in the price level, resulting from the increase in government expenditure, reduces the real value of the stock of money and shifts the *LM* curve along the *IS* curve (seen as a movement along the *AD* curve) to a lower level of income than would have prevailed in the absence of the reduction in the real quantity of money.

Crowding out will be total with a vertical *LM* curve. This occurs, for instance, when the demand for money is interest inelastic. In this case an increase in bond-financed government expenditure will only affect the interest rate and not the level of income. In the case of bond-financed expenditure when there is a budget deficit, however, unless the government reduces the deficit (by cutting expenditure or increasing taxation), bond holdings in the private sector will continue to increase. This situation is illustrated in Figure 7.8. As long as this continues, the increase in the bond stock will increase private sector wealth, which will lead to an increase in the demand for money (a leftward shift of the *LM* curve). This may push real income back to Y_0. If an increase in bond holdings also constitutes an addition to wealth that leads to an increase in consumption, the *IS* curve will also shift further to the right.

Of course the ultimate effect of bond-financed fiscal policy on the level of real income will depend on the relative sizes of the shifts in the *IS* and *LM* curves. It is conceivable that bond-financed fiscal policy is both expansionary and contractionary. If the initial effect of government expenditure increases income but the later effects through wealth are stronger on the *LM* side, then the policy will turn from expansionary to contractionary.[3]

The contraction caused by wealth effects is likely to diminish over time if we assume that bond-financed fiscal policy is expansionary even though bonds represent net additions to wealth in the private sector. In this case the expansionary effect on income will increase tax receipts (income taxes), which will ultimately reduce the budget deficit.

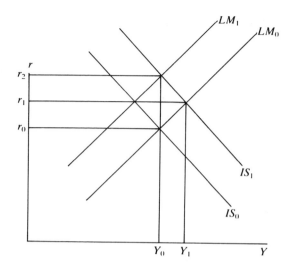

Figure 7.8   The effect of bond financed government expenditure on the rate of interest and income level

In the case of an increase in government expenditure that is curves shift), wealth effects on consumption will shift the *IS* curve further to the right. Even in this situation there could be a wealth effect on the demand for money if it is argued that as wealth accumulates (money and bonds) more spending will take place but also individuals will wish to hold more money, causing a rise in the demand for money. The *LM* curve will then shift to the left.

Crowding out also occurs because public expenditure may be a direct substitute for private expenditure. In this case if the government provides goods and services that the private sector requires, then the private sector will simply undertake a corresponding amount of private saving. In this case crowding out is voluntary since it requires no relative price or wealth effects to set it off. It is likely to be stronger for investment in public utilities than, for example, in infrastructure where public investment may actually lead to an increase in private investment, particularly for manufacturing.

7.8 Expectations and demand management

The framework so far developed for policy does not allow for the expectations of individual firms about future fiscal actions. Incorporating expectations into the framework will affect the predictability of fiscal policy's impact on the level of real income. Individuals will have expectations of what the effects of fiscal policy are on the future value of economic variables, and these expectations will in part determine their current behaviour. By incorporating these expectations, the reaction of individuals to policy changes may be different to that anticipated by the government. In our analysis, this implies that some of the behavioural relationships underlying our framework may change.

The outcome of these effects arising from expectations and perceived changes in wealth depend to a large extent on whether or not future changes in policy are anticipated. If the private sector has widely fluctuating expectations about future policy, then the effects of their actions, shown, for example, through changes in consumption and investment behaviour, are difficult to predict. The government could reduce some of this uncertainty if it announced changes in advance and ensured that individuals had confidence that the government would pursue the policies announced. This would reduce uncertainty and make the effect of changes in monetary and fiscal policy on current real income less ambiguous.[4]

7.9 Monetary and fiscal policy in developing countries

It should be clear from the analysis so far that it is difficult to predict the precise effect that an expansionary or contractionary policy will have on the income level, the price level and the rate of interest. The policy maker must not only identify the appropriate type of policy that will have the correct *directional* effect on the variables it is intended to change, but must also be in a position to assess the relative size of the effect that each policy has on those variables.[5] The relative effect of each policy will depend on the slopes of the AS curve and the IS and LM curves (and correspondingly the AD and RR curves), and the BP curve in the case of the open economy. We now turn to the shape of the curves that may face policy makers in developing countries, and then proceed to examine the use of fiscal and monetary policy in an open economy framework. The *IS* curve is likely to be quite steep in developing countries. The low elasticity of investment demand, particularly in the short run, would tend to increase the slope of the *IS* curve.[6] Enterprises finance their investment expenditure either by borrowing or by using their retained earnings. The level of retained earnings an enterprise is able to secure each year is related to a number of widely varying factors, including the variation in the other costs that the enterprise has to face, such as wage costs, the cost of imported materials and the interest costs of previous loans, particularly as enterprises in developing countries often rely heavily on borrowed funds for working capital purposes. Changes in interest rates, money wage rates and the exchange rate will lead to a change in the variable costs faced by different enterprises, and so these variables will enter the firm's cost function. The relation between variable costs and retained earnings is postulated in Figure 7.9, which shows that retained earnings increase as variable costs fall.

In developing countries, retained earnings, particularly among smaller enterprises, may represent a significant source of investment finance, and therefore if variable costs rise (as interest rates, wages or the cost of imported materials rise), investment will suffer. The interest rate may still be important for smaller enterprises, not

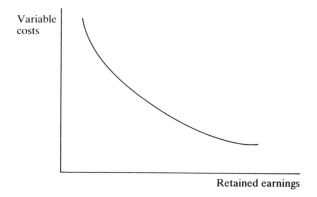

Figure 7.9 Relation between an enterprise's variable costs and retained earnings

necessarily as a decision variable for borrowing, but rather for lending in the informal money sector where interest rates may be considerably higher than the rates in the formal financial market (and risks correspondingly higher).

A large proportion of fixed investment finance, particularly for the larger firms, takes place through state-owned development banks and financial institutions rather than through commercial banks. Since these typically operate in uncompetitive markets, the interest rate is often not the most important variable for allocating investment finance. When investment credit is limited by the government, other criteria become more important such as preferred customers or priority sectors, or the size of collateral. These features reinforce the view that the investment schedule will be quite interest inelastic.

The other components of the *IS* curve, the consumption (and saving) function and the import and export functions may have more moderating effects on the slope of the *IS* curve. The marginal propensity of labour to consume is high in developing countries. A high overall marginal propensity to consume will tend to decrease the slope of the *IS* curve.[7] Further aspects of the consumption function incorporating individuals' expectations about their future income as well as current disposable income are discussed in the appendix to this chapter.

Earlier (see Chapter 5) the *IS* curve was linked to the international sector through the impact of relative price changes P/P_w, where P represents the domestic price level and P_w the price level for the rest of the world. The price elasticity of export supply will be low (particularly for primary products) owing to short-term capacity constraints. In general, as will be discussed in Chapter 8, substitutability between domestically produced goods and imports is low because the latter consist largely of intermediate and capital goods not found in developing countries. Obviously this situation will vary significantly between countries. For these imports, income elasticity of demand is likely to be around unity, with imports increasing in proportion to the growth in overall real income, and price elasticity low.

In the financial sector, several points can be noted. First, the ratio of financial assets, including money, is low in relation to GNP as compared to industrialised countries. Second, as discussed in

Chapter 4, the banking structure is relatively underdeveloped and compartmentalised, with commercial banks providing credit for consumers and working capital finance for enterprises, and more specialised financial institutions monopolising the lending of large-scale investment capital through subsidised credit facilities. The demand for money is principally for transactions purposes rather than for speculation in financial markets, which in general are poorly developed or non-existent. A more significant modification to the demand for money relation developed in Chapter 2 is in the types of transaction for which enterprises demand money balances. These include variations in the demand for money required to meet changes in their variable costs (wages, interest costs and imported intermediate goods inputs), which may be particularly interest inelastic. Since the money supply is determined by the government, the demand for money function has a strong influence on the slope of the *LM* curve. The factors described above would indicate that the curve is steep. Combining the factors that influence the shape of the *IS* and *LM* curves implies that the slope of the downward-sloping aggregate demand curve is relatively steep.

We have already seen from Chapter 3 that the aggregate supply curve *AS* is relatively flat but upward sloping below levels of full employment, and this can now be used with a steeper-sloping *AD* curve to examine the impact of monetary and fiscal policy on the price level and output in an open economy.

Figure 7.10 shows that a given change in fiscal policy (a change in government expenditure financed by printing money), by shifting the AD curve to AD_1, will have a relatively larger initial effect on output than on the price level, raising Y to Y_1 and P to P_1. However, the price level will not remain at P_1 since the supply curve will shift leftwards as the cost of production to enterprises is raised as a result of a change in fiscal policy. An increase in government expenditure will raise interest rates, which in turn raises production costs by inflating the cost of financing working capital (a similar effect will be achieved by a change in the exchange rate if it raises the costs of imported intermediate goods). The effect on the price level and output will, of course, depend on the size of the relative shifts in the respective curves. It could, however, be envisaged that the *AS* curve shifts to such an extent as to offset the initial rise in output and push up the price level further to P_2. It is, therefore, a change in

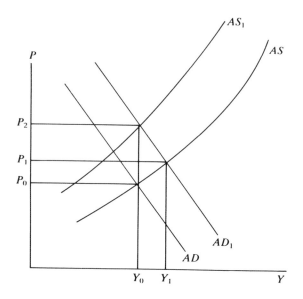

Figure 7.10 The effect of a change in money-financed government expenditure on the price and income levels in a closed economy

aggregate demand working through the supply side of the economy that leads to a rise in the price level.

It now remains to examine the case of a money-financed increase in government expenditure in the open economy framework. As before, an increase in government expenditure shifts the AD curve to the right, to AD_1 in Figure 7.11. We assume that the RR curve remains unchanged as the change in expenditure shifts it to the left and the change in the money supply shifts it in the opposite direction. The initial disequilibrium in the balance of payments (ab) shown with price level P_0 and the rate of interest r_0, rises to cd when the price level is increased to P_1.

Given that the exchange rate and money wages do not change but the rise in interest rates shifts AS to AS_1, the impact on the balance of payments is to worsen the external deficit. (Notice that the interest rate moves up again as further imbalances are caused by changes in the real supply of money. The shift in the AS curve raises the price level, causing a movement along the AD_1 curve.) The balance of payment deficit increases to ef.

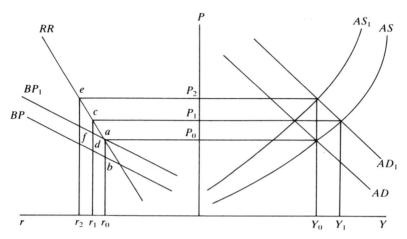

Figure 7.11 The effect of a change in money-financed government expenditure in the open economy

Starting from an initial balance of payments disequilibrium, an increase in money-financed expenditure has worsened the balance of payments position. This topic and the implications for the type of exchange rate policy to be adopted are examined in the next chapter.

Throughout this chapter we have shown some of the difficulties facing governments attempting to influence the level of income. In the case of fiscal policy, although it may be a relatively easy option to resort to the printing press to finance government expenditure, it may not in all cases represent the preferred policy in terms of its effects on prices, income, rate of interest and balance of payments. Other options do exist in the form of financing government expenditure by increasing taxes or by encouraging the private sector to hold government debt. If these latter two options prove difficult to accomplish, then financing the budget deficit through printing currency will ensure that the budget deficit becomes a permanent and even a dominant component of the monetary base.

Further reading

An excellent treatment of up-to-date theory and stabilisation policy dealing with industrialised countries is found in Stevenson, Muscatelli and Gregory (1988). A useful textbook which discusses some of the dilemmas facing policy makers in developing countries is contained in Killick (1981). Porter and Ranney (1982) compare monetary and fiscal policy in a 'standard less developed country model' with 'a standard advanced country model'. On stabilisation see Crockett (1981), Leff and Sato (1980) and Dornbusch (1982), and for the effects of financial liberalisation in developing countries see Dooley and Mathieson (1987). An up-to-date discussion of recent country experience into financial liberalisation in Asia is given in Cho and Khatkhate (1989). A wide range of factors influence the domestic savings rate. In this book the level of income has been an important factor. For a review of the savings literature that examines the influence of interest rates and social security variables see Polak (1989). This work also looks at the role of private domestic saving in relation to domestic investment, and examines the effect on this when the government is a net dissaver and when there is significant capital flight. On government finance in general see Goode (1984).

Appendix: Permanent income hypothesis

The marginal propensity to consume may be smaller than indicated in this chapter if account is taken of the permanent income hypothesis.

Permanent income is defined as the income individuals expect to receive on the basis of their wealth, occupation and ability. Expectations are formed on the basis of past experience and from observations of what individuals earn in similar circumstances. Consumption may also be defined in a similar way. Permanent consumption is, then, the consumption that a person expects or plans to make. Actual or measured income and consumption may be larger or smaller than permanent income and consumption.

Actual or measured income and consumption is divided into permanent and transitory elements. If measured income is higher (lower) then permanent income, then the transitory component, which explains the difference, will be positive (negative).

The transitory elements are not considered permanent enough to change the way people perceive their permanent income. A poor harvest, for instance, will result in a negative transitory component of income. However, transitory consumption is not correlated with transitory income and therefore, although a poor harvest results in actual income with a negative transitory component, consumption will not be reduced. Similarly, in the case of 'windfall' increases in transitory income (say an export boom), the *MPC* relating to this income is also zero. Since consumption is unaffected by transitory changes in income, being instead determined by longer-run considerations, all changes are reflected in an increase in savings.

The implications for our original consumption behaviour of an *MPC* from transitory income that is zero are that the *MPC* out of measured or actual income is unstable. The value of *b* in our earlier consumption function is therefore not constant. Whenever income changes and individuals perceive the change to be transitory or temporary, then the *MPC* (i.e. the effect on consumption) will be small.

Notes

1. Again the money supply may be changed by a combination of changes in the other variables.
2. In this case the consumption function can be respecified to include changes in the stock of money.
3. Although our analysis is essentially short run, there is considerable debate about whether bond-financed expenditure carries a future tax liability since there is an obligation on the part of government to pay interest and capital. If this is the case and bond holders perceive this tax liability, then the bonds will not represent a net addition to their wealth and hence the effects on the *LM* curve will be lessened.
4. Economists have tried to formalise the part played by expectations by considering expectations as an endogenous element in the analysis.
5. The directional effect is associated with specifying the correct functional relation between variables, i.e. $C = f(Y)$, while the size effect relates to the functional form, i.e. the relative slopes of curves.
6. The reader can verify the effect that an inelastic investment schedule has on the *IS* curve by constructing a vertical investment demand curve in the four quadrant diagram in Chapter 2 and replotting the *IS* curve.
7. The diagram below is constructed on the basis of two savings functions (representing $MPC = 0.6$ and $MPC = 0.8$). Joining each quadrant as we did in Chapter 2 shows the change in the slope of the *IS* curve.

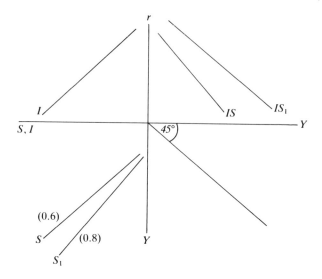

8

Exchange rate and balance of payments policy

In this chapter we consider policy to deal with external imbalance. A key policy instrument at the government's control is the exchange rate, and the choice of the 'right level' for the exchange rate is a critical decision in an open economy. In Chapter 5 we saw how a change in the price of imports or exports would affect the trade balance. It is now necessary to examine more carefully the conditions under which these changes will occur.

8.1 Exchange rate determination

The exchange rate is the price of one currency in terms of another. Most countries define their exchange rate as the price of a foreign currency (typically the US dollar) in terms of domestic currency units (e.g. rupees). Like any other commodity, the price of a currency is determined by the supply of and demand for it. That is, if the supply of a currency exceeds the demand for it, its price falls, or if demand exceeds supply, the price rises. In Figure 8.1, the exchange rate is determined by the domestic country's demand and supply of the foreign currency, with the equilibrium rate of 100.

Now suppose our economy is in external imbalance, with a balance of payments deficit. This means that the demand for dollars exceeds the supply, and can be shown in Figure 8.1 by an exchange rate of 80. One way of removing the imbalance in the foreign exchange market would be to change the exchange rate to the

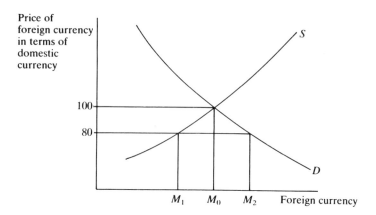

Figure 8.1   The foreign exchange market

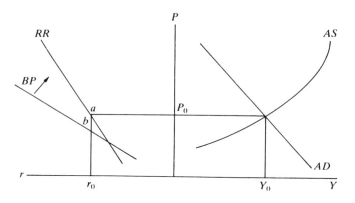

Figure 8.2   Internal equilibrium with a balance of payments deficit

equilibrium level of 100. This is called *devaluation*, since it reduces the value of a unit of domestic currency relative to foreign currency (or increases the value of foreign currency in terms of domestic currency). The imbalance in this market is also reflected in the balance of payments deficit shown in Figure 8.2.

With internal equilibrium achieved (below full employment in this example) with Y_0, P_0 and r_0, the resulting balance of payments deficit is shown by ab. A devaluation will shift the BP curve rightwards to reduce the gap between *a* and *b*. The detailed effects of this change on other variables will be examined later in the chapter.

8.2 The causes of balance of payments disequilibrium

Many developing countries are confronted by the problem of balance of payments disequilibrium, which manifests itself in an external account deficit. How does this come about?

The international economic environment is highly volatile, and is the source of major external shocks to developing countries. Shocks in the goods market can arise from exports and imports. The demand for exports is heavily influenced by the level of economic activity in the main industrial countries, and a recessionary downturn will lead to a fall in export earnings. Where a country relies heavily on exports of a few commodities, changes in demand for these products, which may be unrelated to trends in the overall state of the world economy, can have a serious impact on the country's trade balance. Export shocks are represented in Figure 8.3 by a leftward shift of the supply curve, which means that the existing exchange rate does not balance the trade account.

What we now need to consider is whether a devaluation of the

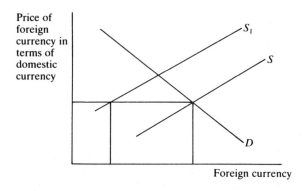

Figure 8.3 The effect of an export shock in the foreign exchange market

exchange rate will correct the trade deficit and restore equilibrium in the trade account. There are a number of distinct processes by which devaluation can help to restore external balance.

8.3 Elasticities approach

The elasticities approach concentrates on the effect of exchange rate changes on the trade balance. To begin with, we will assume that all goods and services are tradable, i.e. are potential exports or imports, including import competing goods and services.

In Chapter 5 we assumed that the demand for imports depended on the level of income and the ratio of domestic and foreign prices. The demand for exports was also related to the same price ratio. If a country devalues, the domestic price of imports will rise and the foreign price of exports will fall. Demand for imports will fall and demand for exports will increase. The impact of these changes in the demand for exports and imports on the demand and supply of foreign exchange (e.g. dollars) depends on the elasticities of demand for the traded goods. If the demand curve for imports is downward sloping, the foreign exchange payments for imports will fall, i.e. demand for dollars declines. The more price elastic the demand for imports, the larger the reduction in foreign exchange demand. If demand for domestic exports is elastic, total foreign currency expenditure, and therefore the supply of foreign currency, increases; but if foreign demand is inelastic, total foreign currency expenditure, and therefore the supply of foreign currency (dollars) falls. The impact of devaluation on the trade balance depends, therefore, on the combined result of the change in import and export demand.

This result can be presented more formally in terms of the *Marshall–Lerner* condition, which gives the critical values of demand elasticities for devaluation to increase the balance of trade. This condition is that: the absolute sum of the two demand elasticities (exports and imports) must be greater than one. Strictly, this condition depends upon two other conditions being met – the elasticities of supply of exports and imports should both be infinite, and the initial position of the trade account should be balanced.

The elasticities approach has provided the basis for a longstanding debate between 'pessimists' and 'optimists', with the former

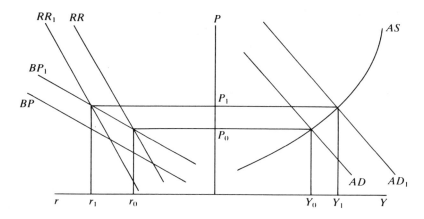

Figure 8.4 The effect of devaluation in a flexible wage model below full employment

arguing that demand elasticities are so low as to prevent devaluation working to improve a trade deficit. This argument has been made more forcefully in relation to developing countries. On the import side, it is argued that most imports are essential items, with limited possibilities for substitution of domestic goods. The elasticity of demand for imports is therefore extremely low. If the country produces a major share of world exports of a primary product, demand elasticity for exports will also be low.

The elasticities approach is useful in identifying the importance of price competitiveness as a determinant of export and import demand. However, by concentrating solely on the effect of devaluation on the trade balance, it ignores the additional repercussions of an exchange rate change on the goods and money markets, and hence on the economy's internal balance. If devaluation is successful in improving the trade balance, there will be a net increase in the level of domestic expenditure or absorption. This is illustrated in Figure 8.4 by the rightward shift in the AD curve.

The economy is in internal equilibrium at Y_0, P_0 and r_0 and has a balance of payments deficit indicated by the BP curve intersecting the RR curve at a point below the internal equilibrium level. A devaluation will improve the balance of trade, and the net increase in demand raises real income. As incomes rise, import demand also rises, but since the price of imports has also risen, domestic producers will increase their output by competing more effectively with imports in the domestic market. As a result the balance of payments improves, shown by a rightward shift of the BP curve, and aggregate demand is increased, shown by a rightward shift of the AD curve to AD_1 and a leftward shift in the RR curve to RR_1. Real income has risen to Y_1, and the price level and rate of interest have risen to P_1 and r_1. Real income has increased via the multiplier effect after taking into account changes in prices and the interest rate. The increase in domestic output raises imports, and the improvement in the trade account is smaller than the initial devaluation-induced improvement.

If the domestic economy is already at the full capacity level of output, a devaluation cannot improve the trade account unless it is accompanied by a reduction in domestic expenditure. This can clearly be seen in Figure 8.5, which shows that devaluation again lowers the price of domestic goods relative to the rest of the world, and leads to a shift in the AD curve. This time, however, the economy is in full employment, shown by the AD curve intersecting the AS curve on its vertical part. Although BP shifts as the exchange

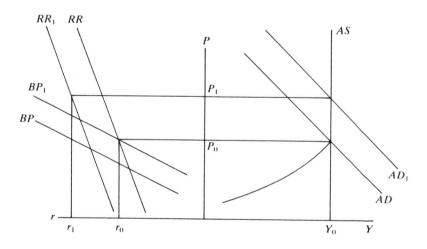

Figure 8.5   The effect of devaluation in an economy with full capacity

rate is changed, the deficit is not improved. The full effect of devaluation is reflected in the increases in the domestic price level and the interest rate, but real income or output is left at Y_0. Only by reducing domestic demand can output be made available to meet the increase in export demand. In other words, unless there is spare capacity available, as in Figure 8.4, devaluation on its own will be insufficient to improve the balance of payments. This leads to the absorption approach to the balance of payments.

8.4 Absorption approach

To demonstrate the link between the elasticities and absorption approaches to the balance of payments, it is useful to introduce the concept of non-traded goods. We continue to assume that the domestic prices of the traded goods are determined in world markets, translated into domestic currency values by the exchange rate. The internal market for non-traded goods is in equilibrium, but there is an external imbalance, with excess demand for traded goods giving rise to a trade deficit.

How can this external deficit be removed? One option is to reduce aggregate expenditure by fiscal measures. This will reduce the domestic demand for exportables and so increase the supply of exports. At the same time, the demand for imports will fall. The net effect would be a reduction in the excess demand for tradables and a reduction in the trade deficit. However, the reduction in total domestic absorption will also lead to a fall in demand for non-traded goods. The non-traded goods sector's initial equilibrium will be disturbed and excess supply will emerge.

How will the excess supply of non-traded goods be eliminated? Following devaluation, the price of traded goods will rise relative to that of non-traded goods. The result will be twofold: the demand for non-traded goods which can substitute for imports will increase; and the resulting change in relative profitability will draw resources out of non-traded production and into the production of traded goods, thereby increasing the supply of exports.

The full effect is illustrated in Figure 8.6. This shows the initial effect of a change in the exchange rate on prices and the rate of interest. The AD and RR curves shift from AD to AD_1 and RR to RR_1 respectively. Real output remains at Y_0. The use of fiscal policy

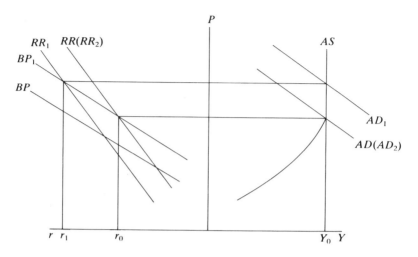

Figure 8.6   Devaluation and domestic absorption

to reduce the level of aggregate demand will result in a shift of the AD curve in the opposite direction, to AD_2. The RR curve also moves in the opposite direction, from RR_1 to RR_2. The balance of payments deficit is only reduced as a result of a reduction in the level of aggregate demand, with the final change in the BP curve (BP_1) intersecting RR_2 to provide internal and external equilibrium.

We see, therefore, that to achieve the targets of external and internal balance two key instruments are needed. To deal with a balance of payments deficit, devaluation is needed to generate the change in domestic relative prices that is required to improve the external balance. A reduction in domestic absorption is also needed to maintain internal balance. Neither instrument alone is sufficient to achieve both internal and external balance.

From our earlier discussion of supply conditions, we know that the increased supply of traded goods in response to the change in relative prices is conditional upon labour accepting a fall in real wages. If money wages rise in response to the rise in traded goods prices, the effect of devaluation will be negated. In the same way, if the prices of non-traded goods are raised, the relative price change effect of devaluation will be eroded.

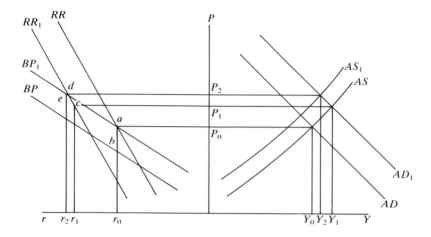

Figure 8.7 The effect of a change in the fixed money wage in the open economy

The effect of a change in money wages is shown in Figure 8.7. Following the initial devaluation and the corresponding shifts in the AD, RR and BP curves, money wages rise in response to the rise in the price level from P_0 to P_1. The effect of a change in the money wage is to shift the aggregate supply curve AS (refer to Chapter 3) to the left. This will raise the price level to P_2 and reduce output to Y_2. Since there is no further change in the AD curve, just the movement along AD_1 as the price level increases, there is no shift of the RR curve. Interest rates increase as a result of changes in the real supply of money reflected in a movement along RR_1. This means the balance of payments deficit shown by ab is not now rectified (shown by point c) and reappears as a deficit indicated by de.

The analysis of devaluation in terms of traded and non-traded goods is shown diagrammatically in Figure 8.8. The economy's output is divided into traded (T) and non-traded (N) goods. The production possibilities frontier is PP. The relative prices of traded and non-traded goods is given by the slope of GG. GG also shows the possible combinations of total expenditure on domestically produced goods (i.e. $C + I + G + X - M$). This expenditure is equal *ex-post* to national income (Y).

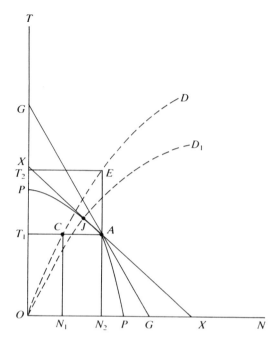

Figure 8.8   The impact of devaluation and absorption on traded and non-traded goods

Domestic absorption is expenditure by domestic residents, and is equal to $C + I + G$. OD shows combinations of T and N demanded at each level of absorption. If the trade balance is in deficit, absorption will exceed income.

In Figure 8.8 total expenditure and income, in terms of traded goods, is OG, but absorption is OE. The non-traded sector is in equilibrium at A, with demand and supply of non-traded goods equal to N_2. The difference between demand for and supply of traded goods is therefore $T_2 - T_1$. Suppose we try to correct the trade deficit by demand management, i.e. expenditure reduction, alone. Absorption has moved down the line OD to point C. At C the demand for and supply of traded goods are equal, but there is excess supply of non-traded goods ($ON_2 > ON_1$). The restoration of balance of payments equilibrium has created disequilibrium in the non-traded sector.

Now suppose we devalue the exchange rate. This is seen as a shift in the price line to *XX*. This alters the price ratio of traded and non-traded goods, and production shifts from non-traded towards traded goods. In Figure 8.8, production shifts from *A* to *J*. The devaluation also affects the combination of traded and non-traded goods demanded at each level of absorption. Since the relative price of traded goods has increased, the demand for non-traded rises. The *DD* curve therefore moves to the right to *DD*₁, and the policy of demand reduction shifts demand from *E* to *J*. To achieve balance of payments equilibrium therefore requires a fall in absorption and a devaluation.

8.5   Monetary approach

The monetary approach to balance of payments concentrates on the overall balance of payments, rather than just the trade account. It stresses the role of monetary changes in the adjustment of external imbalance, and argues that much of the adjustment will be an automatic process. The basic model rests on a number of assumptions: that output consists of traded goods only, that output is at the full employment level, and that the demand for money function is stable. The relationship between the demand for and supply of money is the key determinant of movements in the balance of payments.

Suppose we begin with a situation of internal and external equilibrium. The demand for and supply of money are equal, and the external sector is in balance. Now suppose the money supply increases as a result, say, of increased government borrowing from the Central Bank. The supply of money now exceeds the demand for money, and households and firms begin to accumulate surplus cash balances. Under the monetary approach the demand for money remains unaltered, since income has not changed, and households therefore increase their expenditure in an effort to restore their money balances to the optimal level (remember this process was discussed in Chapter 7). Since output is already at full capacity, the increased demand is met by increased imports and the balance of payments moves into deficit. The creation of excess money balances has resulted, therefore, in a balance of payments deficit.

The balance of payments deficit will tend to be corrected by the automatic adjustment mechanism. Under a fixed exchange rate, a balance of payments deficit results in a loss of reserves. As we have seen, reserves form part of the money supply base, so the reserve loss will lead to a fall in money supply, reversing the process initiated by the original expansion in the domestic component of the total money supply.

The monetary approach is perhaps best viewed as a long-run adjustment process which draws attention to the importance of monetary changes for the correction of balance of payments disequilibrium.

But what are the implications of the monetary approach for the use of devaluation as an instrument for short-run adjustment in the external balance? The analysis is similar to the traded and non-traded process already described, except that the adjustment is in terms of monetary variables rather than the real side adjustments of the elasticity and absorption approaches.

As before, devaluation raises the relative price of traded goods. Since the demand for money is expressed in real terms, an excess demand for money emerges which induces domestic economic agents to reduce their expenditure in order to increase their money balances. At the same time, the increase in the relative price of traded goods encourages producers to reallocate resources from non-traded to traded goods. The reduction in expenditure on imports and the increased supply of exports create a balance of payments surplus which matches the excess demand for money. Through time, the inflow of reserves increases the money supply, and equilibrium in the money market and the balance of payments is restored.

In this analysis, devaluation creates a temporary balance of payments disequilibrium by disturbing the equilibrium between money demand and supply. The excess demand for money created by the devaluation necessarily improves the balance of payments. But the improvement is temporary and only lasts for as long as it takes for equilibrium in the money market to be restored.

Why should a country wish to devalue if monetary adjustments will ensure that equilibrium will be restored in the balance of payments? One reason may be that the country has insufficient foreign reserves to finance a balance of payments deficit while moving back to equilibrium. Alternatively, when a country is in balance of payments equilibrium, devaluation might be used as a means of increasing foreign reserves.

8.6 Devaluation and the capital account

In Chapter 5 we saw how international capital movements are influenced by the relationship between domestic and foreign interest rates: if there are no restrictions on the movement of capital in and out of the economy, a fall (rise) in the domestic interest rate with foreign interest rates remaining unchanged will lead to an outflow (inflow) of capital. We can add a further determinant to the flow of international capital by suggesting that it will also be influenced by expected changes in the exchange rate. If a devaluation is anticipated, capital flight (a sudden outflow) will occur in order to avoid the losses that a devaluation would bring. If capital flight occurs on a large scale and resources are limited, government will need to increase its foreign borrowing in order to obtain the necessary foreign exchange with which to meet the demand for outward remittances, i.e. to sustain its balance of payments position. As the volume of capital outflow increases, so the pressure for devaluation is intensified, and the size of the devaluation which is finally undertaken will be larger than would have been required before the flight began. The devaluation instrument is now being used to influence both the trade and the capital accounts, but the magnitude of the exchange rate change needed to correct the imbalance in each account may differ.

Suppose the policy makers are faced with a trade deficit and growing capital account deficit caused by capital flight. To correct this overall balance of payments disequilibrium the exchange rate is devalued and at the same time domestic interest rates are raised. The increase in interest rates coupled with the removal of uncertainty about exchange rate changes may encourage a reversal of the capital flight, as capital flows in again. If the inflow is not sterilised and the domestic money supply increases, there will be demand pressure for exchange rate revaluation. But an appreciation of the exchange rate, resulting from short-term capital inflow, will reduce competitiveness in the goods sector and make recovery in the trade account more difficult. The solution to the problem is to assign an additional policy instrument to the objective of protecting the domestic economy against large-scale, short-term speculative movements of international capital. Controls on international capital flows are used by many developing countries for this purpose. This allows the policy maker to use the exchange rate solely as the instrument assigned to the trade account.

8.7 Nominal and real devaluation

So far we have assumed that non-traded goods prices do not increase with devaluation. Devaluation is effective, therefore, in altering the relative prices of traded and non-traded goods, which in turn generates the desired improvement in the trade account. But costs will often increase following devaluation. The increased cost of imported inputs may be passed on in higher prices of non-traded goods. If labour is resistant to a fall in real wages, money wages may rise to compensate for the increase in the domestic price of traded and non-traded goods.

A rise in the prices of non-traded goods erodes the increase in competitiveness obtained by devaluation. To measure changes in competition it is useful to redefine the exchange rate in real terms. The *real exchange rate* is measured as

$$RER = ER \times \frac{P_{US}}{P_d}$$

where ER = nominal, or official, exchange rate (rupees per dollar),
P_{US} = US price deflator,
P_d = domestic price deflator.

The higher the nominal exchange rate, and/or the higher the rates of US prices to domestic prices, the more competitive is the domestic economy in trade with the United States.

Many variants of the real exchange rate are possible, using different price indices. In line with the traded/non-traded goods analysis of devaluation, an alternative definition of the real exchange rate is

$$RER = ER \times \frac{\text{price of traded goods}}{\text{price of non-traded goods}}$$

Since a country will trade with many countries, it is often necessary to express the nominal exchange rate as an average of a 'basket' of exchange rates of the country's major trading partners. This gives an *effective exchange rate*. If we also allow for price level movements in the country concerned and its trading partners, we can calculate a *real effective exchange rate*.

8.8 Exchange rate arrangements

So far we have discussed how a policy-induced devaluation of the exchange rate can work to correct an external disequilibrium. Looked at from the other end, we could interpret an external deficit as evidence of exchange rate misalignment, requiring devaluation to restore external competitiveness. How can a country avoid exchange rate misalignment? Are there any types of exchange rate policy that will minimise the likelihood of overvaluation and a balance of payments deficit?

Unfortunately there is no single or straightforward answer. A variety of different types of exchange arrangement are possible, ranging from more or less permanently fixed rates to freely floating rates.

Currency peg

Under this arrangement a country fixes its currency against another currency, usually that of its dominant trading partner. This has the advantage of insulating the economy against movements in the prices of goods traded with its major trading partner. However, the country's effective exchange rate may become unstable if the exchange rate of the major currency to which the country has pegged moves against other major currencies. A variant of the currency peg which is commonly used is to peg the domestic currency to a basket of currencies, whose weights reflect the share of the countries in foreign trade. This reduces the fluctuations in the effective exchange rate. On the other hand, it is quite possible that the bilateral rates against each of the currencies in the basket will fluctuate. International trade and financial transactions are carried out in terms of bilateral rates, and therefore face the risk that these rates will be unstable since under a basket peg the domestic currency is not pegged to any of the foreign currencies used for financing transactions.

Floating exchange rate

An alternative to the currency peg arrangement is to have a fully flexible, or floating, exchange rate. Here the rate is allowed to adjust instantaneously to any imbalances between demand and supply, removing the need for reserve movements. There are, however, major disadvantages with this type of arrangement. The uncertainty associated with fluctuating exchange rates creates the need for a well-developed financial system which can provide traders with forward cover against exchange rate movements. Few developing countries possess such a financial infrastructure. Second, if the price elasticities of traded goods are low, export and import values will be slow to respond to an exchange rate change, and the exchange rate may spiral up or down rather than fluctuating around a trend. In some countries, the violent movements in the exchange rate may be moderated by short-term speculative capital movements, but experience suggests that, where such capital movements do occur, they are often in the wrong direction, simply reinforcing the instability in the exchange rate.

Controlled exchange rate

Given the disadvantages of both the fixed and flexible exchange rate arrangements, an attractive option might be to select an in-between arrangement, exercising some control over movements in the exchange rate. A *crawling peg* arrangement allows for changes in the single- or basket-pegged exchange rate, to allow for relative movements in domestic and foreign trading partners' price levels. Here the authorities are aiming at holding the real effective exchange rate constant, maintaining a constant position in the country's 'price competitiveness'. This is a relevant target for economies, and in the next chapter we will see how a major overvaluation of the real exchange rate (which occurs if the domestic inflation rate exceeds the foreign rate) can have a major depressing effect on the domestic market as well as on trade performance.

A *managed float* commits the authorities to intervening in the foreign exchange rate to regulate the speed of the market's adjustment in bilateral exchange rates. Where the country operates a basket arrangement, the authorities are aiming to reduce fluctuations in the nominal effective exchange rate.

8.9   Exchange rate changes as a policy instrument in developing countries

Devaluation has been widely used as a policy instrument in developing countries and has been a key element in stabilisation programmes. At the same time its use has been a controversial issue, and many observers have argued that the structural features of developing countries render devaluation an ineffective tool for dealing with a balance of payments disequilibrium. In this section we will consider some of the ways in which the structural character-istics of a 'typical' less developed country can influence the impact of an exchange rate devaluation on the economy's internal and external balances. Three examples will be used. The first looks at the 'elasticities debate'. The second examines the impact of devaluation on the level of real income. The third uses the tradable–non-tradable framework to show how a failure to realign the exchange rate in response to changes in the external account can contribute to serious sectoral imbalances (the 'Dutch disease' phenomenon).

The elasticity debate

In the earlier discussion of the elasticities analysis of devaluation we pointed out that some commentators have argued that the elasticity conditions that need to be fulfilled if devaluation is to improve the trade balance are unlikely to be met by developing countries. The condition for successful devaluation was given by the Marshall–Lerner condition, that the sum of the elasticities of demand for exports and imports should be greater than one. The value of these elasticities will be determined by the economy's structural charac-teristics. On the side of imports, the demand elasticity will tend to be low if the economy's productive structure is heavily dependent on essential imported inputs. The process of import-substituting industrialisation followed by many developing countries has shifted the composition of the import bill away from consumer goods towards intermediate and capital goods, and has tended to lower the economy's aggregate import elasticity. On the side of exports, the demand elasticity will be affected by the composition of exports. The pessimists argue that many developing countries are unable to expand export sales without lowering price, and that inelastic foreign demand means that total foreign exchange earnings will decline if price is reduced.

The Marshall–Lerner condition is based on two restrictive assumptions: that the supply elasticities of exports and imports are infinite, and that the trade account is initially balanced. What happens if we relax these assumptions?

Most developing countries account for a minor share of total demand for the imported commodity, and a change in demand is unlikely to have much effect on the supply price. The assumption of infinite elasticity of import supply is reasonable, therefore, for most less developed countries. But many LDCs are exporters of primary and agricultural products, the supply of which cannot easily be increased in the short run. The supply elasticity of exports may therefore be quite low. This will reduce the likelihood of devaluation improving the trade balance.

To see why this is the case, consider the example of a country which has zero elasticity of export supply and zero elasticity of import demand. In Figure 8.9 devaluation initially lowers the foreign price of exports from P_0 to P_1. If the market structure is competitive, the excess demand for exports will force the price to

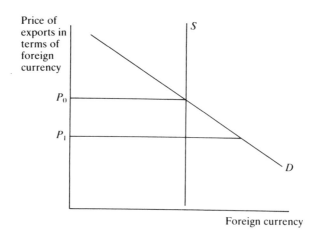

Figure 8.9   The effect of devaluation under different market conditions

rise back to the pre-devaluation level P_0. In this case, the foreign exchange receipts of the exporting country remain unchanged by devaluation. If the market is oligopolistic, however, the buyers may be able to 'negotiate' with the suppliers to sell at a price of P_1. In this case, exporters' foreign exchange receipts decline. Now consider what happens on the side of imports. Since the demand elasticity is zero, demand does not respond to the higher domestic price of imports, and total expenditure of foreign exchange is unaltered. Thus, we see that devaluation will, at best, leave the trade balance unchanged, but could result in a worsening of the trade account.

If we consider the previous example in terms of the domestic currency, then devaluation will worsen the trade balance. Domestic income receipts for exports remain unchanged, but domestic expenditure on imports increases. If the devaluation occurs in a position of initial deficit, the deficit is magnified by the devaluation.

To summarise, the traditional elasticities analysis of devaluation assumes high supply and demand elasticities, which together ensure that the devaluation produces an improvement in the trade balance. However, these high elasticities imply certain underlying structural characteristics in the economy. Where, as in many developing countries, the structural features are very different to those assumed in the orthodox analysis, the elasticities condition for successful devaluation may not be met, and exchange rate changes can produce a 'perverse' movement in the trade balance.

The contractionary impact of devaluation

Critics of devaluation as a policy instrument in developing countries have pointed to the potential adverse macro-level effects. Consider once again the case of an economy with zero domestic export supply and import demand elasticities. Devaluation in this situation worsens the trade deficit, valued in local currency terms. If devaluation occurred with an initial deficit, the widening of the trade deficit has an immediate deflationary impact, since the increase in the domestic currency value of the deficit constitutes a leakage from the income stream ($Y = C + I + G + X - M$: an increase in the deficit between X and M lowers Y). Since domestic output does not respond to devaluation, the devaluation does not have the effect of raising income. At the same time, devaluation has

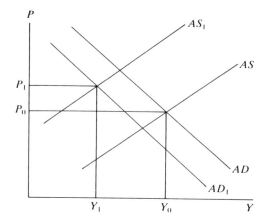

Figure 8.10   The supply-side effects of devaluation

a further deflationary impact by lowering the domestic absorption level. This can occur through several mechanisms.

First, devaluation may lower absorption through its redistribution effects. If devaluation raises prices, but nominal wages are unchanged, there is a shift in income from wages towards profits. If profit receivers have a lower consumption propensity than wage earners, the overall level of absorption falls. A second mechanism by which devaluation may lower absorption is the real balance effect. The price rise following devaluation lowers the real value of cash balances, and expenditure is reduced in order to raise real money balances back to the desired level.

The contractionary impact of devaluation may also work through cost-push effects on the aggregate supply side of the economy. Devaluation increases the local currency cost of imported goods, and raises producers' costs. The effect is identical to imported inflation or domestic cost shocks, and can be represented by a leftward shift of the aggregate supply curve. As discussed earlier, a devaluation-induced increase in the price of final goods and services is likely to provoke a response from labour as it attempts to defend its real standard of living against inflation erosion.

The impact of devaluation in an economy with the structural features described above is shown in Figure 8.10. For a given price level, devaluation has a contractionary impact on absorption, resulting in a leftward movement of the AD curve to AD_1. This is caused by the redistribution and real balance effects (i.e. a leftward shift of the IS and LM curves leading to a leftward shift in AD). At the same time, the aggregate supply curve shifts leftwards to AS_1, since devaluation directly increases variable costs of production. The combined effect is a major reduction in output from Y_0 to Y_1, and an increase in the price level from P_0 to P_1. We now have a diagrammatic representation of the structuralist critique of devaluation in developing countries, i.e. that it will be stagflationary, with output falling and prices rising.

The Dutch disease effect

One of the most significant economic occurrences of recent years was the dramatic rise in oil prices in the 1970s, following the formation of the OPEC producers' cartel. Similar large increases in world prices occurred for several primary commodities, notably coffee. For the producer countries, these export price rises resulted in a massive and sudden increase in foreign exchange earnings. Here we examine how an export 'boom' affects a country's exchange rate and macro equilibrium, and how policy could be designed to adjust to this type of exogenous shock.

The term 'Dutch disease' was adopted to describe a phenomenon first observed in Holland when the extraction of natural gas from the North Sea began. The Dutch disease occurs when the exploitation of a natural resource is accompanied by a fall in output in other sectors of the economy.

We can analyse the Dutch disease phenomenon using a three sector model of a small open economy. There are three sectors: the booming sector (e.g. oil) which exports all its output, the manufacturing sector and the non-traded sector. The economy therefore produces two traded outputs and one non-traded output. What happens when there is a 'boom' in the oil sector? The initial effect is to raise incomes in this sector, which leads to increased domestic demand for both traded and non-traded goods. The additional demand for traded goods is met by increased imports. For the non-tradables the shift in demand will lead to a rise in prices, so that the price of non-traded goods relative to that of traded goods increases. This causes resources to shift away from tradable goods.

The rise in non-tradable goods prices leads to an appreciation, or loss of competitiveness, in the real exchange rate (recall that the real exchange rate was defined earlier as the nominal rate multiplied by the ratio of tradable goods prices to non-tradable goods prices). This lowers the relative price of imported goods, while export prices rise for foreign consumers. This exacerbates the shift in domestic demand and productive resources from the manufacturing sector to the non-tradable sector, and gives rise to what has been labelled 'de-industrialisation' in the advanced industrialised economies. But the declining sector need not consist only of manufacturing industry. In the oil-producing developing countries, such as Nigeria, Indonesia and Mexico, the agricultural sector will be producing tradable goods, and it is agricultural performance that will be harmed by the Dutch disease effect.

We can illustrate these effects in Figure 8.11, which is similar to Figure 8.8. In the pre-boom period, equilibrium occurs at A, with the economy producing T_1 of tradables (manufactures) and N_1 of non-tradables. Since the line OD shows the combination of T and N demanded at each level of absorption, absorption and income are equal at A. Now suppose the export boom occurs and total export earnings increase. This increases the availability of tradables, so the production possibility frontier shifts from PP to P_1P. If the prices of traded and non-traded goods remain unchanged, the production point moves from A to B. But with the income generated by the export boom, demand will be at C, where the demand for non-tradables, N_2, is greater than supply, N_1.

If the excess demand for N causes the price of non-tradables to rise, and brings about an appreciation of the real exchange rate, the slope of the relative price line P_N/P_T alters to P'_N/P_T. The change in relative price shifts the pattern of demand towards tradables, and the absorption line OD shifts in an anticlockwise direction to OD_1. At point E both tradable and non-tradable sectors are again in equilibrium, with income and absorption equal. Compared with the pre-boom situation, the output of non-tradables has increased (E lies to the right of A). To measure the post-boom output of manufacturers, we take the point on the original production frontier vertically below E (remember that the outward shift of the production frontier was due entirely to increased output of the booming commodity). The output of the manufacturing (or non-boom tradable good) sector has fallen.

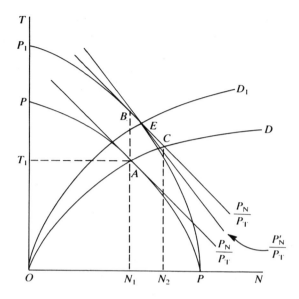

Figure 8.11 The adjustment process following an export boom

What is the problem? The process of adjustment we have described is exactly what we proposed earlier when we discussed the role of exchange rate changes in facilitating domestic resource movements between tradable and non-tradable goods. The reason why so much concern has been expressed about the Dutch disease phenomenon is that the process of adjustment to a boom situation may not be reversible when the boom ends. The re-expansion of the non-oil tradable sector may be very difficult if the basic capital stock and infrastructure have been destroyed. Re-entering export markets will also be difficult as other economies will have captured the market surrendered during the country's boom period. Therefore, since booms in export earnings are likely to come to an end in the not too distant future, it may be sensible to undertake economic policies to protect the manufacturing sector from the adverse effects of the boom.

What should the policy maker do to protect the manufacturing sector? One option is to try to prevent the exchange rate appreciation. If the nominal exchange rate remains unchanged, the trade account balance will improve with an inflow of foreign reserves. To prevent this leading to increased spending, the authorities can undertake sterilisation operations, keeping the supply of reserve assets constant by buying the foreign exchange from the commercial banks and paying for it in non-reserve assets such as government bonds. Alternatively, the government may try to sell its debt directly to the private sector, by raising interest rates. However, this may attract foreign capital inflows and create further pressure for exchange rate appreciation. If the foreign exchange receipts are in the hands of government – the government may own the booming sector – the increase in reserves can be used to reduce a budget deficit.

The main objection to a policy of moderating the exchange rate appreciation in order to protect the non-boom tradables sector is that it leads to an accumulation of foreign assets, in the form of foreign exchange reserves or foreign bonds that the government has purchased with its increased reserves holdings. In effect, the real income gains to the economy from the boom are shifted from the present to the future. This strategy may be effective in the short run, but over the longer term, pressures will build up for the benefits to be passed on in real consumption gains to the economy.

An alternative way of protecting the manufacturing sector is to provide direct subsidisation to the sector's output. This could be tackled by direct government expenditure and investment in the affected sector, perhaps financed by taxes on the booming sector's income. This has the advantage of allowing the non-tradable and booming sectors, and the exchange rate, to adjust to the exogenous export earnings shock.

We have now seen how the effectiveness of the exchange rate as a policy instrument in developing countries will be affected by the structural characteristics of the economies concerned. We have already made the point that each country has a unique set of structural features, and the impact of the policy instrument on the economy's macro performance will differ from country to country. What we have shown, however, is how the basic analytical framework developed in the early chapters can be used to derive predictions as to the impact of policy changes on economies with differing structural characteristics.

Further reading

The student should read the seminal work of Mundell (1962). An extensive treatment of the real exchange rate as a major policy tool in developing countries is to be found in Dornbusch and Helmers (1988). Morley (1988, ch. 7) gives a useful discussion of the traded–non-traded goods analysis. The import and export functions for developing countries are discussed in Khan (1974). For a general discussion of exchange rate misalignment the reader is referred to Bird (1983) and Edwards (1988). For issues concerning capital flight see Cuddington (1986), and for Dutch disease see Corden (1984).

9

Inflation policy

Most of the analysis so far has been developed without a discussion of the problem of inflation. Changes in the economic variables have therefore been expressed in real terms. Where price changes were allowed to occur, as, for example, in the discussion in Chapters 2 and 3 of the effect of a change in aggregate demand when the aggregate supply curve is upward sloping, we looked at the effect in terms of a once and for all change in the price level. Similarly, in the discussion of devaluation, we analysed the impact of a given price increase on the structure of relative prices. However, we know that inflation, which we define as a continuous increase in the price level, is endemic in many developing countries. The task of this chapter, therefore, is to identify the policy instruments that can be used to control inflation.

9.1   Inflation and aggregate demand

Figure 9.1 reproduces Figure 3.10, and shows that an increase in the aggregate demand curve from AD to AD_1 leads to a rise in the price level. The rise in the price level is caused by the upward slope of the aggregate supply curve. From the analysis in Chapter 3, we know that the slope of the aggregate supply curve is related to the underlying behavioural characteristics of the labour market. In particular, if labour supply is responsive only to changes in real wages, the aggregate supply curve is vertical, but if labour is willing

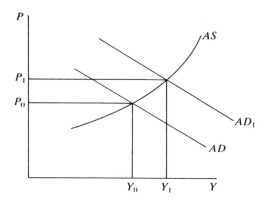

Figure 9.1 An increase in aggregate demand

to supply in response to an increase in labour demand, even though the real wage has fallen, then the supply curve is upward sloping. In other words, it is the assumption that labour does not react to a fall in real wages by withdrawing its labour, at least in the short run, that provides the upward-sloping *AS* curve. We can modify the analysis slightly by assuming that labour will be increasingly less willing to tolerate a fall in real wages, the closer the economy is to a full employment position. This suggests that, as full employment is approached, the slope of the aggregate supply curve increases and eventually becomes vertical at full employment.

The price rise resulting from an increase in aggregate demand is unlikely, in practice, to be a once only increase. It is more realistic to assume that, as demand rises, the rate of increase in prices (i.e. inflation) will increase.

The relationship between the level of demand and the rate of change in money wages was first analysed in the late 1950s. It was assumed that the rate of change of wages varied positively with the amount of excess demand in the labour market.

In Figure 9.2 there is excess demand for labour at money wage W_0: our assumption about the dynamic adjustment process means that the larger the size of this excess demand, measured by $L_0 L_1$, the more rapidly W will move towards W_e. This is represented in Figure 9.3.

If we substitute the level of employment for the excess labour

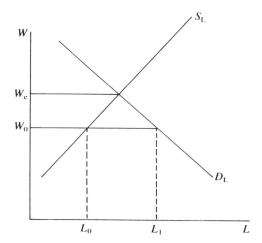

Figure 9.2 Adjustment in the labour market

demand function, Figure 9.3 can be represented in Figure 9.4, where OA is the level of unemployment which is associated with normal turnover in the labour market (frictional unemployment), and therefore represents a position of labour market equilibrium. Figure 9.4 is generally referred to as the Phillips curve.

Finally if we assume that the rate of change in prices will be the same as the rate of change in money wages, then we have a relationship between the rate of change in prices ($\Delta P/P$), which is the inflation rate, and unemployment. (This assumption depends on producers passing on rising wage costs in higher prices, and in this way keeping their profit margins unchanged.)

There was ample empirical confirmation of the Phillips curve relation during the 1950s and 1960s, but in the late 1960s and the early 1970s many economies experienced increasing rates of inflation with high unemployment. How can we explain the apparent breakdown in the Phillips curve relationship? One influential argument emphasised the role of inflationary expectations, which had been ignored in the original analysis. The observant reader will have noted that Figure 9.2 was not the same as the labour market diagram used in Chapter 2: Figure 9.2 draws the labour demand and supply curves as functions of the *money* wage rate, whereas in Figure 3.5 the schedules are related to the *real* wage

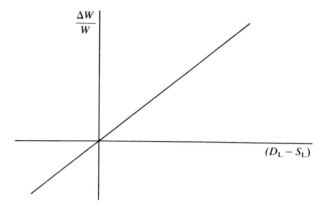

Figure 9.3 Excess labour demand function

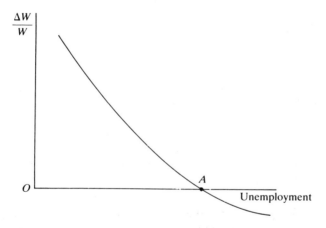

Figure 9.4 Relation between a change in the wage rate and unemployment

rate. If we revert back to the assumption used in Chapter 3, the amount of excess demand for labour will determine the rate of change of real wages, not that of money wages. Can we relate the rate of real wage change to the rate of inflation?

The link between inflation and real wage changes can be made using the concept of inflation expectations. Both employers and employees are concerned about future movements in the price

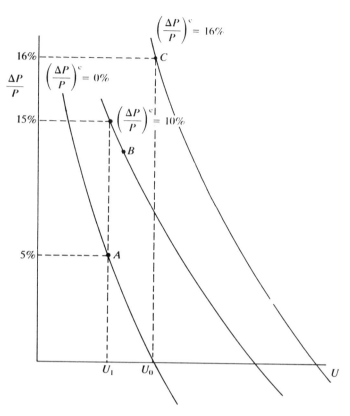

Figure 9.5 Expectations-augmented Phillips curve

level. Both sides of the labour market therefore work out what they think will happen to prices over the period for which they have to make contracts on wages and employment. In other words, they form expectations which are fed into wage agreements. Suppose that some level of unemployment U_0 would be associated with a rate of change in money wages of $(\Delta W/W)_0$. If 10 per cent inflation is expected, then U_0 will be associated with a money wage change of $(\Delta W/W)_0 + 10$ per cent. This means that there will be a series of 'expectations-augmented' Phillips curves, each associated with a particular inflation rate. In Figure 9.5, for example, the lowest Phillips curve is linked to zero expected inflation $(\Delta P/P)^e = 0$, and the next curve is for expected inflation of 10 per cent. The vertical distance between the two curves is equal to the difference between the expected inflation rates, i.e. 10 per cent.

Suppose that unemployment is at level U_0, which is associated with $\Delta W/W = 0$ on the $(\Delta P/P)^c = 0$ curve (the expectations-augmented curve): inflationary expectations are confirmed as correct. But at levels of unemployment to the left of W_0, wage changes and inflation are above zero, so expectations are not fulfilled. Suppose that unemployment is at U_1, and this is associated with money wage and price increases of 5 per cent on the $(\Delta P/P)^c = 0$ curve. On the second Phillips curve, U_1 is associated with inflation of 5% + 10% (the vertical distance between the curve), and inflationary expectations are not met.

What happens when the government attempts to lower unemployment from U_0 to U_1 by increasing the level of aggregate demand? Initially unemployment falls as output rises in response to the demand stimulus, but at the same time, money wages increase. At U_1 employers and employees realise that their inflation expectations ($= 0$) have been too low, and therefore in the next round of wage negotiations they build in their inflationary expectations, say 10 per cent. This pushes up the inflation rate, and also begins to erode the 'real' increase in output and employment, so that the economy moves from A to B in Figure 9.5. Expectations again turn out to have been too low, and the process is repeated with the economy shifting to another higher Phillips curve. The economy adjusts along the path ABC and reaches equilibrium at C, when unemployment is back to its original level U_0 and actual and expected inflation are equal.[1]

This analysis suggests that the long-run Phillips curve is a vertical line through U_0 and that the trade-off between unemployment and inflation exists only in the short run. The long-run unemployment equilibrium is U_0 (described as the natural rate of unemployment). If unemployment falls below U_0, inflation increases; if unemployment increases above U_0, the inflation rate falls.

A similar analysis can be repeated in Figure 9.6 using the four quadrant diagrams developed in Chapters 2 and 3. Again suppose the government wants to reduce the level of unemployment from U_0 to U_1, shown by the shift in the AD curve from income level Y_0 to Y_1. As a result of the change in the price level from P_0 to P_1, workers demand higher money wages in an attempt to maintain real wages. The wage curve shifts leftwards from W_0 to W_1. This results in a

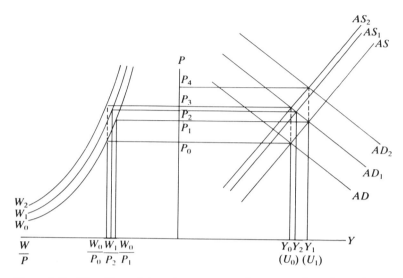

Figure 9.6 The effect of changing aggregate demand and supply on the price level

leftward shift of the aggregate supply curve. If employees' inflationary expectations are wrong (i.e. too low), then prices rise to P_2 and real income lies between Y_0 and the original target level of Y_1. Realising these expectations were incorrect, employees will proceed in the next bargaining round to build in their inflationary expectations, which pushes up prices to P_3 and reduces real income to Y_0. Even within the scope of this analysis it can easily be shown that an inflation spiral might develop. This could occur if the government, after real income was reduced to Y_0, again applied an expansionary policy to shift AD rightwards to maintain income at Y_1 level (U_1 level of unemployment). In this case employees would have to increase wages even further to prevent a deterioration in their real wage.

What are the implications for policy formulation towards inflation control? If we believe in the existence of a Phillips curve relationship, at least in the short run, the control of inflation will depend on a reduction in excess demand in the labour market. But excess demand for labour is in turn determined by an excess level of aggregate demand for goods and services. Here we come up against the assignment problem. If both output (and hence employment) and inflation are target variables, we need at least two policy instruments. Since demand management has already been assigned to the output objective, it cannot be used as an inflation control instrument. Another policy is needed to control wage (and price) inflation. A second policy instrument that can be used is wages policy.

Wages policy could take a number of different forms. The most commonly used approach is where the government seeks the agreement of labour, through the trade unions and employee organisations, to limit the rate of money wage increases in wage bargaining agreements. A wages policy is illustrated in Figure 9.7. Suppose there is inflation due to a rise in aggregate demand.[2] The AD curve shifts from AD to AD_1, raising income from Y_1 to Y_2.

In turn employees are able to bargain wages up in an attempt to compensate for the loss in real wages that occurs as a result of the price level increasing from P_1 to P_2. A change in the money wage from W_0 to W_1 will shift the AS curve to the left, pushing the price level to P_3 and the income level back to Y_3. If the government now imposes a wage policy by keeping wages at W_0, the effect will be to lower the price level to P_* ($P_* = P_2$). This occurs because aggregate supply is greater than aggregate demand at price level P_3 after money wages have been reduced. At this price level (P_*), output is

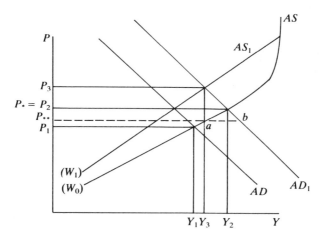

Figure 9.7 The effect of a wages policy on the price and income level

increased from Y_3 to Y_2. With money wages restrained at W_0, real wages have been reduced. Since money wages have fallen by more than the drop in the price level, the increase in output comes about as a result of enterprises expanding employment in response to the real wage decline.

If wage restraint can be adopted, it means that a given level of excess demand will be linked to a lower inflation rate: in other words, the original Phillips curve will move downwards and to the left. If we allow for price increases occurring independently of wage increases, then it will be desirable to extend wages policy to prices and wages policy, with employers agreeing to limit their price increases to an agreed ceiling level.

The effect of controlling both wages and prices can also be shown in Figure 9.7. A proportional reduction in the price level and the money wage is achieved at P_{**} and money wage W_0. With these levels, output is reduced to Y_3, but there is now excess demand shown by the points a and b. This policy can only be sustained by some kind of accompanying measure that reduces the level of aggregate demand.

In terms of the expectations-augmented Phillips curve, the prices and incomes policy may lower expectations and enable the economy to move down to a lower inflation–natural unemployment point on the vertical Phillips curve. It may also be possible to lower expectations by 'talking down' inflation, creating a shift in public opinion towards a lower expected inflation rate.

Wages policy may also be applied more generally to shift the underlying structure of the labour market. Measures to improve labour availability, for example, will tend to lower the inflation rate associated with a given employment level.

9.2 Cost-push inflation

So far we have examined how inflation can arise from short-run movements in the level of aggregate demand. Inflation may also arise, however, from exogenous sources, i.e. from factors that are not closely connected to the economy's aggregate demand and supply position. These sources of inflation are collectively referred to as 'cost-push' factors.

The simplest way of explaining cost-push inflation is to think of the price of an individual good as consisting of the cost of materials used, the cost of labour, and profits (we will ignore indirect taxes and subsidies). The cost-push explanation of inflation assumes that firms set their prices to give a constant mark-up above costs, in this way holding their profit margin constant. With mark-up pricing maintaining constant profit margins, any change in the cost of material inputs or labour will lead to a rise in price. These cost changes are therefore regarded as the cause of inflation.

The cost of imported materials will rise if there is inflation in the rest of the world, and if the domestic exchange rate remains unchanged. For economies which depend heavily on imports of goods used as inputs in production, e.g. oil, imported inflation is an important source of domestic inflation. In the case of labour costs, the cost-push approach to inflation stresses wage increases that occur independently of changes in the level of aggregate demand in the economy. Institutional or sociopolitical forces are seen as 'pushing up' the price of labour. Again a wages policy, broadly defined to cover changes in the underlying structure of the labour market, could be used to deal with cost-push wage increases.

9.3 Inflation and the money supply

In Chapter 2 we saw how a change in the price level altered the position of the *LM* curve. With inflation, the real money supply falls and the *LM* curve continuously shifts. In Figure 9.8 an increase in the price level from P_0 to P_1 shifts the *LM* curve to the left from $LM_0(P_0)$ to $LM_0(P_1)$. This, as we have seen, raises the interest rate and lowers the output level from Y_0 to Y_1.

It now seems that inflation will tend to lower the level of real output. This contradicts the prediction of both the Phillips curve, where a higher inflation rate is linked to a rise in the level of economic activity (associated with lower levels of unemployment), and the cost-push analysis, where prices can rise independently of changes in the level of demand. How can we reconcile these different predictions? The answer lies in considering the government's money supply policy.

If the cost-push or Phillips curve predictions about the relationship between real output levels and inflation are to hold, we have to posit some process by which the money supply increases in

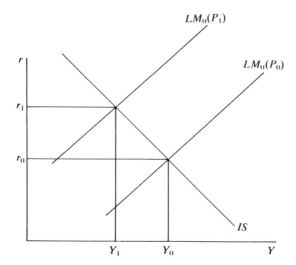

Figure 9.8 Effect of inflation on the LM curve

response to inflation. If, for example, the government wishes to leave income at Y_0 in Figure 9.8, it can increase the supply of money so as to shift the *LM* curve represented by $LM_0(P_1)$ back to its original position, where the real money supply is unchanged since both prices and nominal money supply have increased by the same amount. In this case the original $LM_0(P_0)$ curve becomes $LM_1(P_1)$. In the same way, to achieve a movement along the Phillips curve towards lower unemployment (and higher inflation) will require an expansion in the money supply. Thus the growth in the money supply is caused by inflation, rather than being a cause of inflation.

An alternative mechanism by which the money supply may respond to inflation is through the impact of inflation on the government's budget deficit. If the government has to increase the budget deficit just to maintain its real level of expenditure (i.e. if nominal expenditure is rising faster than nominal tax revenue), and if the authorities do not increase their borrowing from the private and commercial bank sectors, then the money supply will increase to cover the increased deficit.

Similarly, if the supply of bank credit is 'demand led', with the Central Bank permitting the commercial banks to adjust their lending to market demand, and if cost-push inflation causes firms to borrow more to cover their increased working capital costs, then the Central Bank will have to increase the supply of reserve assets to the commercial banks to enable them to fulfil their obligations.

Thus, an important implication of both the excess demand and cost-push views of inflation is that the money supply is endogenous to inflation. An increase in the supply of money is an accommodating condition for inflation, but it is not the cause of the inflationary process.

9.4 The monetarist view of inflation

The main components of the monetarist analysis of inflation have already been discussed in earlier chapters, and we need therefore only draw these various parts together. The monetarist approach starts with the fundamental idea of equilibrium in the money market. The demand for money is a function of the level of economic activity (transactions) in the economy. The supply of money is a function of the reserve asset stock. Now consider what happens if an initial equilibrium in the money market is disturbed by an increase in money supply caused by the Central Bank releasing reserve assets. Firms and households now have excess money balances, which they try to reduce by increasing expenditure on goods and services. Since the monetarist approach assumes that domestic output does not respond to an increase in demand (in other words, the economy is assumed to be at the full capacity output level), the increase in expenditure forces up the prices of the goods being demanded. In the open economy framework it also draws in imports. The increase in prices raises the demand for real money balances until equilibrium in restored with the increased level of money demand equal to the quantity of money. In the open economy, the adjustment is speeded up by the loss of reserves resulting from a trade deficit, which reduces money supply (assuming, of course, that these effects are not sterilised).

The important point to note at this stage is the implication of the monetarist approach for the choice of policy instrument to control inflation. The appropriate instrument to be assigned to inflation control is the money supply. We can also note that in the monetarist analysis changes in the money supply cause inflation, and the causal chain between money supply and inflation is a reversal of that assumed in excess demand and cost-push analysis.

9.5   Inflation policy in developing countries

Inflation is a problem endemic in many developing countries, and it has generated much debate on the causes and appropriate policy 'cures'. The initial debate centred on the high-inflation experience of Latin America in the mid-1950s, and led to the development of the structuralist approach to inflation analysis. This approach was part of a structuralist school which was concerned with the more general problems of underdevelopment. The structuralist approach was juxtaposed with the 'orthodox' or 'monetarist' analysis of inflation.

The structuralist approach incorporates a variety of ideas and concepts, and it is difficult to give a straightforward definition that would encompass this range of arguments. There are, however, two elements which are of particular importance to the discussion of inflation. The first distinguishing element in the structuralist analysis is the rejection of the notion of an economy-level market for each good and factor of production, where market disequilibria are corrected by the response of demand and supply to price changes. In contrast, the structuralist argues that the typical developing economy is characterised by segmented markets, with each segment having its own demand and supply and price relationship. Many markets have two additional features: inelastic supply ('bottlenecks') and limited linkages to other markets for the same item. The results are twofold. First, it is quite possible to have a range of various prices for a given item, say labour, rather than a single market price. Second, inelastic supply and poor integration mean that a given shift in demand is likely to produce a large change in price, rather than an increase in supply.

The second characteristic of the structuralist analysis is to distinguish between the 'proximate' and 'fundamental' causes of inflation. The proximate determinants are the direct causes of inflation, whereas the fundamental determinants of inflation are the factors which themselves bring about the occurrence of the proximate determinants. It is the latter that the structuralists seek to identify. Thus, structuralists may agree with the 'orthodox' analysis that, for example, an increase in money supply is a necessary condition for inflation to occur, but they would try to identify the pressures that led the government to adopt an expansionary money supply policy. The search for the fundamental causes of inflation leads the structuralist analysis back to the underlying economic, social and political structural characteristics of the underdeveloped economy.

We can now consider some of the ways in which the structural characteristics of less developed economies act as inflationary forces. Our approach will be to treat the three main analytical models developed earlier – excess demand, cost-push and monetary expansion – as proximate causes, and to relate these to the underlying structural causes of inflation.

The labour market

The labour market used in our analysis so far has assumed a single national market. In reality, the labour market in developing countries is characterised by different segments, with workers being paid different wages depending on the sector of the economy in which they are employed. There may well be a modern urban sector in which money wages are unresponsive to shifts in demand, and alongside it a traditional or informal sector where returns to labour are highly flexible. This wage dualism may be the result of various institutional factors. Minimum wage laws may cause wages to be higher than they would otherwise be. Labour unions, pay policy for public sector employees, and multinationals' pay (high wages may be paid to create goodwill and avoid expropriation) will all have the same effect of offering wages which are higher than market clearing in the 'modern' segment of the labour market. In contrast, in the 'informal' sector (self-employed, unorganised workers), returns to labour are highly flexible and are more likely to be determined by market forces.

The interaction between these two segments of the labour market is illustrated in Figure 9.9. Assume prices are constant at P_0. Institutional factors in the formal sector hold the real wage at W_1/P_0, which is above the market clearing wage W_0/P_0. The excess supply of labour shifts into the informal sector, with the consequence that wages in that sector are forced below the level that

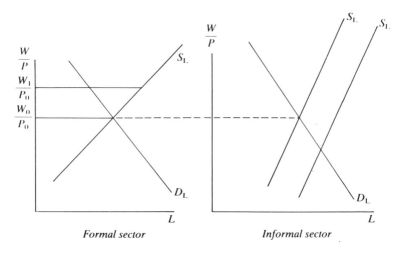

Figure 9.9   The labour market with a formal and informal sector

would have arisen in a totally unrestricted labour market. If entry into the informal labour market is unrestricted and there are no constraints on the demand side, full employment will be achieved by the movement of labour from the formal to the informal sector.[3]

An important characteristic of these dual sector models is full employment. Any worker who does not gain employment in the high-paying sector is assumed to relocate to the low-paying sector and to find an income-generating activity there. In the absence of social security support, workers cannot afford to be unemployed for any length of time, and they are therefore prepared to work for much lower wages (or returns per unit of effort) in order to generate sufficient income to support themselves. In Chapter 3 we saw how the shape of the aggregate supply curve depended on labour market conditions, i.e. on whether money wages were flexible or inflexible. By assuming that money wages were inflexible in a downward direction but flexible in an upward direction, particularly as employment approached the full employment level, an upward-sloping aggregate supply curve was derived.

Thus, if we characterise the structural features of the labour market in developing countries in terms of a two sector model, with fixed money wages and an excess supply of labour in the modern sector, the *AS* curve will be relatively flat. This implies that shifts in aggregate demand are unlikely to lead to major inflationary pressures.

Indexation of wages in the formal sector may be a further feature of the institutionally fixed money wage situation assumed in Figure 9.9. 'Indexation' refers to any system of automatically changing prices of various kinds (exchange rate, wages, interest rates, etc.) to take account of changes in the general level of prices. Full indexing will maintain real values. The problem is that if there is an exogenous price shock to the economy, through, for example, a rise in the price of imported goods, the indexation of wages will mean that money wages will also increase, reinforcing the upward movement in the general price level.

Even in the absence of indexation, an exogenous price increase can lead to wage-push pressures. Imported inflation erodes labour's real disposable income. If labour organisations are strong enough to react, they will try to defend their members' real standard of living by increasing nominal wages. A process of oligopolistic bargaining between labour organisations and employer groups can quickly develop into a wage–price inflationary spiral, with each side attempting to avoid a fall in its real income and expenditure levels.

Production relations and non-labour inputs

A major source of inflation in developing countries is likely to be non-labour cost-push factors. An increase in the cost of imported inputs or domestically produced materials will increase the cost of production and is likely to be passed on in price increases through the use of mark-up pricing.

In Chapter 3 we used a simple aggregate production function which described the technical relationship between the output of goods and services and a single input, labour. It was assumed that in the short run output could be increased by simply applying more labour to the fixed stock of capital. In this section we will modify this assumption and allow for the structural features of production in a 'typical ' developing country. The implications of these structural characteristics for inflation will then be discussed. In many less developed countries there is significant under-utilisation of the capital stock. This can occur for a variety of reasons. Intended under-utilisation occurs when there are distortions in the relative prices of labour and capital. Minimum wage legislation, for example, raises the price of labour relative to that of capital; controls which put a ceiling on interest rates will have a similar distorting effect. If the price of capital assets is kept relatively low, then producers will have less incentive to utilise them fully. Unintended under-utilisation occurs where various structural features of the economy prevent producers from reaching their target level of capacity. To understand how this can occur we need to modify the assumption of Chapter 3 of only one variable input in production. In reality, a short-run increase in output will usually involve increased use of not just labour, but also working capital and other material inputs. If the supply of any of these inputs cannot be increased, then an increase in output is blocked by this 'constraint'. Some relaxation of this type of input constraint might be obtained by altering the mix of inputs used in production, but the opportunities for this kind of substitution are limited. Many production functions are characterised by fixed or near-fixed factor proportions, which means that the inputs must be increased in a fixed proportion if output is to be raised.

One of the main arguments made by the structuralist school is that many developing countries are subject to a foreign exchange constraint. The growth in foreign exchange receipts is insufficient to meet rapidly growing import demands generated by economic growth. Production technology is typically imported from abroad, and is therefore relatively intensive in its use of imported inputs for which domestic substitutes are not available. The result of the foreign exchange bottleneck is that production is constrained below the full utilisation level by the limited availability of necessary imported inputs. The same effect on capacity will arise if there are bottlenecks or supply constraints in domestic inputs, such as power, transport or skilled labour.

The effect of capital stock under-utilisation and input supply constraints will be to change the position and slope of the aggregate supply curve. This is shown in Figure 9.10. The original production function PF_1 in the SE quadrant was drawn on the assumption of full capital stock utilisation. If there is under-utilisation of capital, the production function becomes PF_2. This converts the aggregate supply curve from AS_1 to AS_2. The effect of a variable input constraint can be shown by a change in the slope of the production function. A given change in the input of labour will now produce a

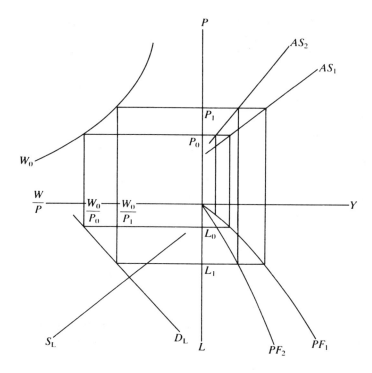

Figure 9.10   The effect of capital stock under-utilisation on the aggregate
supply curve

lower marginal product due to the limited availability of the other
necessary inputs.

The use of imported inputs can also act as a conduit for imported
inflation. A rise in the price of imports will translate into a domestic
price increase if the exchange rate is fixed. In many developing
countries the goods sector is dominated by a relatively small
number of large firms, giving a high degree of producer concentra-
tion. Earlier we argued that mark-up, or administered, pricing is
likely to be the norm in non-competitive markets. The increase in
import costs will therefore be passed on in an increase in output
prices. The effect will be the same as for a cost-push wage increase,
and can be represented by a leftward shift in the *AS* curve.

A further structural bottleneck identified as a fundamental cause of inflation is found in the domestic food-producing sector. The supply responsiveness of the agricultural sector is thought to be low because of structural constraints within the sector. In the Latin American literature these supply bottlenecks were related to the structure of land tenure which prevented producers from receiving the benefits of increased market sales, but they can also arise from bottlenecks in the transport infrastructure, or poor marketing arrangements. The growth of the modern industrial sector increases the demand for food, and with food production unable to respond by increasing supply, the price rises. Imports of food are constrained by the foreign exchange bottleneck. Food is the major element in the urban sector household's expenditure, and the price rise represents a significant reduction in real income standards. Labour therefore presses for an increase in money wages, which can trigger off an inflationary spiral.

A final cost-push factor can be mentioned. In Chapter 7 we examined some of the implications of interest rate controls. In many developing economies, enterprises rely on short-term borrowing to finance their variable input purchases. Interest repayments can represent a significant part of production costs. If interest rates are increased, the cost of working capital is increased, and the aggregate supply curve is again shifted leftwards.

We have now seen how the structural features of a less developed economy can influence that economy's inflation experience. We have done this by relating the fundamental, structural origins of inflation to the proximate causes, and have then shown how the changes in these proximate causes will shift the slope and position of the aggregate demand and supply curves, thereby causing an increase in the price level.

One final point needs to be made. A shift in the aggregate demand or supply curve will cause the price level to increase. However, this is not the same as inflation, which we have defined as a sustained increase in the level of prices. As we saw earlier, a rise in prices will be converted into inflation only if there is an accommodating increase in the quantity of money. The structuralist analysis of inflation seeks to go beyond the superficiality of monetary explanations by explaining the underlying structural forces which result in an expansion of the money supply. An increase in the quantity of money nevertheless remains a necessary condition for inflation.

Further reading

For a general review of inflation in developing countries see Kirkpatrick and Nixson (1987). Segmented markets are analysed in Roemer (1986). Cline (1981) contains a useful collection of essays on developing countries' inflation experience.

Notes

1. This adjustment process depends on the assumption that expectations are formed on the basis of past inflation experience (adaptive expectations). If expectations are formed on the basis of forecasts of future inflation (rational expectations), the short- and long-run expectations-augmented Phillips curves are identical and vertical.
2. The analysis of inflationary tendencies (defined as a continuously rising price level) is difficult to portray using the static analysis framework adopted in this book. The change in aggregate demand in Figure 9.7 must be regarded as a snapshot of a continuing process.
3. A similar analysis could be developed for an urban (high-wage) and rural-subsistence (low-wage) Lewis-type dual sector model. In this case wages are higher in the modern urban sector in order to attract a sufficient pool of labour.

10

Stabilisation policy in developing countries

Stabilisation policy refers to a programme of economic policy measures designed to achieve broad macroeconomic objectives such as an improvement in the growth of real output, a low rate of inflation and a sustainable balance of payments position. According to the International Monetary Fund, the objectives of macro stabilisation policy are 'the restoration and maintenance of viability to the balance of payments in an environment of price stability and sustainable rates of economic growth'. As we saw in Chapter 1, many developing countries have experienced very serious problems in each of these three areas, and as a result have been required to design and implement comprehensive stabilisation programmes aimed at restoring macroeconomic equilibrium in the economy. These stabilisation programmes have frequently been undertaken in conjunction with the International Monetary Fund, which has made its lending conditional on the acceptance of a package of macroeconomic policy measures.

The need for macro stabilisation policy measures arises when there is an imbalance in the economy between aggregate demand and supply. The causes of this fundamental imbalance are many and varied, and it is often difficult to identify the separate influence of these different factors on the economy's macro performance. Often the imbalance originates in external shocks, such as a rise in foreign interest rates, an increase in the price of imports or a decline in the foreign price of exports. All of these factors put immediate pressure on the balance of payments, which in turn can adversely affect the economy's internal price and output levels. Macro disequilibrium may also be caused by domestic factors. An excessive level of aggregate demand, caused by rapid monetary expansion, for example, will lead to inflationary pressures, a reduction in the growth of real output, and balance of payments disequilibrium. Sooner or later these disequilibrium pressures will force a change in economic policy to correct the underlying imbalance between supply and demand. The task of the policy maker will be to design a package of policy measures which will bring the economy back to equilibrium. To do this requires a judgement to be made on what the effects of applying particular policy instruments will be on the aggregate demand and supply levels, and hence how effective they will be in moving the target variables back to their equilibrium levels.

The analytical approach used in the preceding chapters has concentrated on policy instruments that are mainly intended to influence the aggregate demand side of the economy. These policies represent the core of macroeconomic analysis, and demand management has been, and continues to be, the central component of stabilisation policy. However, this does not mean that stabilisation programmes have to rely exclusively on demand-side policies, and there is now a greater recognition on the part of those responsible for the design of stabilisation programmes that supply-side policies can also play a part in restoring macroeconomic equilibrium.

The contribution of 'demand-side' and 'supply-side' policies to the stabilisation objective can be illustrated using Figure 10.1. Assume that the economy is initially in equilibrium at price level P_0 and full capacity output level Y_0. Aggregate demand increases to AD_1 and causes the price level to rise to P_1. If the policy maker relies entirely on demand-side policies, the objective is to shift AD_1 back to AD. But suppose supply-side policies are also used. If successful, these policy measures will increase the volume of real output supplied by the domestic production sector at a given level of aggregate demand. This can be represented by a rightward movement of the aggregate supply curve to AS_1. Therefore, the aggregate demand curve now needs to be reduced only to AD_2 to restore equilibrium: stabilisation is achieved by a combination of demand reduction and supply augmentation policies.

In this chapter we will describe how the application of particular

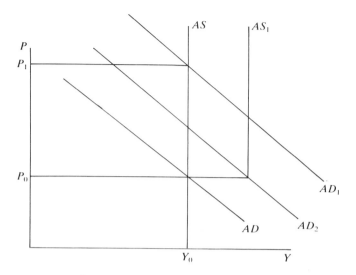

Figure 10.1   Stabilisation with demand- and supply-side policies

policy instruments can be expected to affect the major target variables in a stabilisation programme. We will concentrate on demand management policy, but in the last section we will also consider the role of supply-side management in stabilisation programmes.

The underlying theme of this book is the argument that the impact of particular stabilisation measures on the target variables will vary according to the structural and institutional characteristics of the economy in which the measures are applied. The structural features of many developing countries are very different to those implicitly assumed in the majority of macroeconomics textbooks, and as a consequence the behavioural response of the 'typical' developing economy to a given stabilisation measure may diverge from the predictions derived from the analysis directed at industrialised economies.

Throughout this chapter we will be comparing the 'industrialised country model' with the 'developing country model'. Our two contrasting models consist of elements drawn from a variety of analytical approaches. No single economy is likely to have all the features of either the industrialised or the developing country model, but many economies will display some of the assumed structural and institutional characteristics.

The 'industrial country model' is similar to the analytical framework that underlies the International Monetary Fund's approach to stabilisation policy formulation. The model assumes a small, open economy with a fixed (policy-determined) exchange rate. Markets are largely unregulated and competitive, with movements in market prices bringing about equilibrium between supply and demand. The model incorporates the real and monetary sides of the economy in the adjustment process, but emphasises the monetary mechanisms as the most important element in stabilisation programmes.

The 'developing country model' also assumes a small, open economy with a fixed exchange rate. But in contrast to the other model, markets are regulated and segmented, and often oligopolistic or monopolistic in character. Supply is typically inelastic to price movements, reflecting underlying supply-side constraints. The financial market in particular is underdeveloped, limiting the effective use of monetary policy as a stabilisation tool.

Our distinction between the framework used for analysing 'industrialised' and 'developing' countries is similar to the more familiar dichotomy found in the development economics literature between 'monetarist' and 'structuralist' analysis. We have not used these labels in this chapter, however, to avoid the idea of monetarism *versus* structuralism. The relevant issue in macroeconomic policy in the developing country context is 'what works where and when', and the most appropriate analytical approach will often involve drawing on elements of both industrial country and developing country models. But ultimately the issue of which particular representation of developing countries' structural characteristics and behavioural relationships is most appropriate will be resolved only by empirical evidence on the results of stabilisation policy.

10.1 Demand-side stabilisation policy

Almost all stabilisation programmes contain three major policy measures: monetary or credit contraction, fiscal contraction and devaluation. In this section we will consider how the application of these three policy instruments to the stylised models would affect the target variables of inflation, real output and the balance of payments. Each policy instrument is considered in turn, exploring its effect first in the 'industrialised country' model, and then in the 'developing country' model.

Monetary contraction

The industrialised country model

The policy maker produces a reduction in the level of credit, either by increasing the reserve asset ratio imposed on the commercial banks, or by reducing government borrowing from the Central Bank (the reader is referred to Chapter 7 for a more detailed account of a change in the money supply). From Chapter 4 we know that a change in money supply is made up of changes in its domestic and international components:

$$\Delta M_s = \Delta D + \Delta R \tag{10.1}$$

where M_S represents the supply of money, D is domestic credit, R is international reserves and Δ indicates a change in the relevant variable. The demand for nominal money balances is a function of the level of real income, the rate of interest and the price level:

$$M_D = f(Y, r, P) \tag{10.2}$$

where M_D is the demand for money, Y is real income, r is the rate of interest and P is the price level.

Equilibrium in the money market requires

$$M_s = M_D \tag{10.3}$$

Substituting (10.3) into (10.1) and rearranging the terms, we obtain

$$\Delta R = \Delta M - \Delta D \tag{10.4}$$

$$= f(Y, r, P) - \Delta D \tag{10.5}$$

This expression indicates that the change in foreign assets (R) will be negative (the balance of payments will be in deficit) to the extent that the change in domestic credit exceeds the change in total money supply.[1] Any change in domestic credit expansion above the equilibrium level would therefore result in a one-to-one loss of reserves. A more likely outcome, however, is that part of the disequilibrium in the money market will spill over into output, rate of interest and price changes, lessening the impact on the balance of payments.

The policy-induced reductions in money supply create excess demand for cash balances. In order to restore their money balances to the desired level, individuals either lower their expenditure or sell bonds. The reduction in expenditure on imports improves the balance of payments. If part of the reduction in expenditure occurs in the domestic economy, however, then real output and/or prices fall. This also occurs as bond prices fall and interest rates rise, adversely affecting investment. The balance between the output and price changes will depend on how near the economy was to full employment prior to the reduction in domestic credit. The initial impact of the policy of credit reduction is therefore a reduction in inflation, an improvement in the balance of payments and a fall in real output. The reduction in the domestic price level alters the relative prices of non-tradables and tradables, increasing competitiveness and encouraging expenditure switching, reinforcing the improvement in the balance of payments.

The 'industrialised country model' analysis of internal and external balance adjustment to a policy of monetary contraction is shown in Figure 10.2. Initially the economy is in internal and external equilibrium. In the SE quadrant the money supply is reduced from $LM_0(P_0)$ to $LM_1(P_0)$. The change in the quantity of money means money demand is greater than money supply. Since there is a movement along the downward sloping *IS* curve, interest rates rise initially from r_0 ro r_1. Similarly, there will be imbalance between aggregate supply and demand, resulting in a fall in output from Y_0 to Y_2 and a fall in the price level from P_0 to P_1, shown by the shift from *AD* to AD_1 in the NE quadrant. The *LM* curve will further shift as a result of the increase in the real value of money as the price level falls. This is seen in the change from $LM_1(P_0)$ to $LM_1(P_1)$.[2]

There will, however, be further shifts in the *IS* curve (and correspondingly in the *AD* curve) if the imbalance in the money market causes expenditure changes not related to changes in interest rates or income (remember that as income falls and interest rates rise, expenditure on consumer goods including imports falls, as shown by the movement along the *IS* curve). When this happens

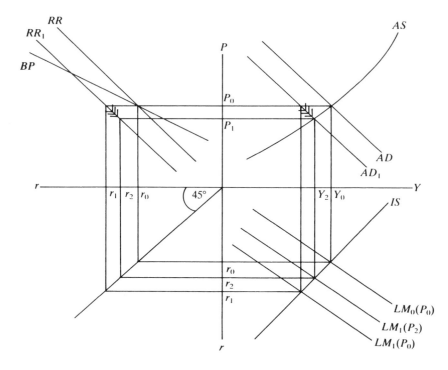

Figure 10.2 Adjustment to monetary contraction in an industrialised country

a new sequence of *LM* curves appear as further price level changes occur during adjustment to the new equilibrium.

The end result is an improvement in the balance of payments, shown by the surplus position in the NW quadrant, as prices are lower and interest rates higher than their initial positions of P_0 and r_0. The impact is twofold, with an improvement coming from the expenditure reduction effect being reinforced by the expenditure switching effect as the domestic price level falls.

The developing country model

Now consider the repercussions of a policy of monetary contraction in a developing country model framework. The government

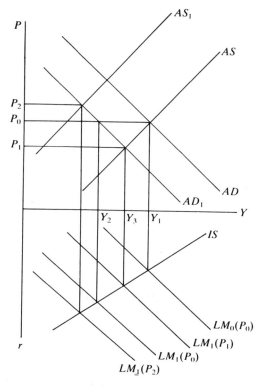

Figure 10.3   Adjustment to monetary contraction in a developing country

reduces the domestic money supply, lowering its borrowing from the Central Bank, or controlling the availability of foreign reserve assets (in the developing country model there are trade and foreign exchange controls). As before, the fall in credit available to the private sector means the demand for money exceeds the supply of money. In the developing country model this excess demand transfers to the informal money market, causing households and firms to withdraw their funds from the market.[3] This causes the informal, unregulated rate of interest to rise, which in turn leads to a decline in investment demand. This is shown in Figure 10.3 by the leftwards shift in the aggregate demand schedule. Downward pressure is put on prices, and provided the aggregate supply curve is upward sloping (recall from Chapter 9 that labour market conditions in developing countries suggest a relatively flat *AS* curve), then the level of aggregate output falls.

An important feature of the developing country model is the assumption that the price level is often determined on a fixed producers' mark-up basis. The increase in interest rates in the informal sector will have an effect on the costs of production through the increase in working capital costs, and producers will mark up prices. This shifts the aggregate supply curve to the left in Figure 10.3. The result is to accentuate the decline in output and to reverse the price level decline that resulted from the downward movement of the aggregate demand curve.

What effect will the policy of monetary contraction have on the balance of payments? If the economy is operating with a disequilibrium (overvalued) exchange rate maintained by trade and foreign exchange controls, then there will already be excess demand for imports, with import rationing. The fall in import demand resulting from the decline in income will lower the level of excess demand, but will leave the actual imports unchanged. The reduction in excess demand may, however, allow the domestic scarcity price of imports to fall.

This adjustment process for import demand and price is shown in Figure 10.4. The exchange rate is controlled at disequilibrium level

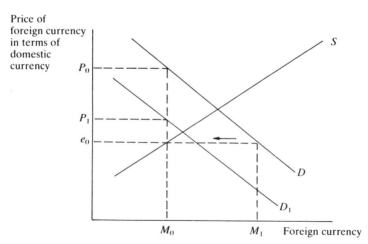

Figure 10.4 Adjustment to monetary contraction on the balance of payments

e_0. There is excess demand for foreign currency $M_0 M_1$. The domestic market clearing price of the available supply of foreign currency (M_0) is P_0. If monetary contraction leads to a fall in real income, the demand for foreign currency schedule shifts to D_1, lowering the domestic price to P_1.

Given the assumed structural characteristics of the LDC model, monetary contraction appears to be an ineffective policy instrument for correcting internal and external disequilibria. The decline in real output may be excessive, the moderation in the inflation rate is offset by the cost-side price increases, and there is no improvement in the balance of payments.

Fiscal restriction

The industrialised country model

A reduction in the fiscal deficit is often regarded as a central policy instrument in altering the level of aggregate demand and external trade balance, and fiscal policy is therefore a key component of most adjustment programmes.

The impact of fiscal policy on aggregate demand will consist of the direct effects of a change in government expenditure and/or revenue position, and the indirect effects which these changes in the fiscal balance have on the private sector's expenditure level.

The direct effect of a reduction in public expenditure is to lower aggregate demand for domestic goods, and/or imports, depending on the pattern of public expenditure between traded and non-traded goods.[4] The indirect effects on private sector spending are less certain. In the industrialised country model, the level of private sector spending tends to move inversely with public sector spending, so that the effect of a restrictive fiscal policy on domestic aggregate demand is small. There are several mechanisms through which private expenditure rises as public expenditure falls. If the public sector supplies goods and services that compete as substitutes with private sector output, the public sector reduction will allow the private sector to increase its share of the market. Second, if the public expenditure reduction is large, the fall in total aggregate demand may lower the transaction money demand, reduce interest rates and, if private investment is interest sensitive, raise investment. If these various 'crowding-out' effects of a change in public

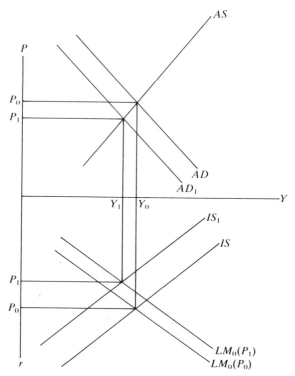

Figure 10.5 The impact of contractionary fiscal policy in an industrialised country

sector expenditure on private sector expenditure occur, then the impact of a contractionary fiscal policy on the internal economy will be limited. This is shown in Figure 10.5 by the small leftward movement in the *IS* and *AD* curves.

What will the effect of fiscal contraction be on the external balance? If a proportion of public expenditure is on imported goods, there will be some reduction in imports. However, when public expenditure is reduced, the cuts are likely to be made in consumption, rather than in capital expenditure, in order to protect the government's longer-term investment plans. Consumption expenditure will consist largely of non-traded services, so the impact on imports will be limited. If public expenditure is cut by reducing foreign borrowing, the capital account of the balance of payment will deteriorate as a result of the expenditure contraction.

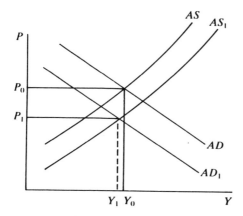

Figure 10.6 The impact of a contractionary fiscal policy in a developing country

The developing country model

The developing country model analysis of fiscal policy also emphasises the impact that a reduction in public expenditure may have on the private sector, but argues that the level of public and private investment will tend to move in the same direction. There are often strong complementarities between public and private capital formation. Increased public investment, for example in infrastructure, acts as a catalyst to private sector investment. An austerity-imposed cut in public investment expenditure will cause private investments to fall as well. The decline in aggregate demand will lead to a fall in the demand for money. Since the official rate of interest is fixed, the excess cash balances are supplied as loanable funds to the informal financial market. The unofficial rate of interest falls. This may lead to some recovery in private investment but, more important, it lowers the interest costs element in production costs, causing the aggregate supply curve to shift rightwards. The developing country model of contracting fiscal policy is shown in Figure 10.6.

This model predicts, therefore, that fiscal policy could be an effective instrument for reducing inflation. At the same time, it points to the danger of 'overkill' in the contractionary impact of public expenditure cuts on real output if the supply side effect is weak.

If foreign trade restrictions are in operation, it is likely that the

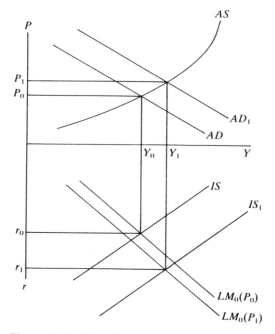

Figure 10.7 The effect of devaluation on the price and income level in an industrialised country

public sector has first choice of the available imports. The cut in public expenditure may therefore lower public sector import expenditure, releasing imports to the private sector, but the overall level of import expenditure is unlikely to fall.

Devaluation

The industrialised country model

The difference between the industrialised and developing country models of devaluation were discussed in Chapter 8 and will therefore only be summarised here.

The industrialised country analysis assumes that the elasticities conditions for successful devaluation are met, and the result is an improvement in the balance of payments. Devaluation has an expansionary impact on the domestic economy, causing demand to rise, and raising output and the price level. This case is shown in Figure 10.7 by the rightward shift in the *IS* and *AD* curves.

If the level of output is increased to full capacity level, the devaluation may need to be accompanied by a policy of expenditure reduction to lower the aggregate level of demand.

The developing country model

In the developing country model it can be shown that the effect of devaluation on the internal balance is stagflationary, and that the external balance will worsen. In Figure 10.8 the *IS* curve shifts to the left as a result of the fall in domestic absorption, and the aggregate demand curve also shifts to the left. At the same time, devaluation

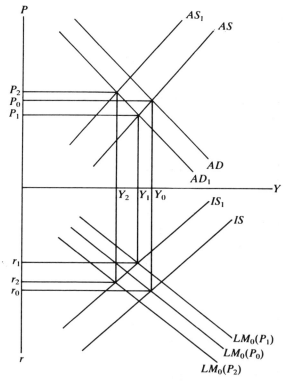

Figure 10.8 The effect of devaluation on the price and income level in a developing country

Table 10.1   Predicted effects of stabilisation policy measures

Policy instrument	Industrialised country model			Developing country model		
	Real output	Inflation	Balance of payments	Real output	Inflation	Balance of payments
Monetary contraction	−	−	+	−	?	?
Fiscal restraint	?	?	?	−	−	?
Devaluation	+	+	+	−	+	?

+ indicates an increase in output and inflation, and a balance of payments improvement
− indicates a fall in output and inflation and a balance of payments deterioration
? indicates an uncertain effect

raises the local cost of imported inputs to production, causing the aggregate supply curve to move leftwards. The effect is a significant reduction in the level of real output from Y_0 to Y_2 and an increase in the price level from P_0 to P_2.

Table 10.1 presents in summary form the predictions derived from the 'industrialised' and 'developing country' models, about the effects of stabilisation measures on the main macro target variables. These predictions have been obtained by assuming a particular set of structural characteristics in each model, and it would, of course, be possible to construct other models for different economic structures which would yield different predictions. What this tells us is that the policy makers must avoid espousal of a single model or analytical framework in designing a stabilisation programme. The appropriate set of policy measures for restoring macro equilibrium to a particular economy will depend upon the structural characteristics and behavioural patterns of that economy.

Although we have considered the effect of each stabilisation policy measure separately, in practice a programme will consist of a package of measures applied simultaneously. This considerably complicates the task of predicting the outcome in terms of the target variables. The speed of adjustment to policy changes differs between different parts of the economy, and these lags make the adjustment process much more complex than has been suggested by our comparative statics approach. An approach to this problem is to construct an economy-level macro model where the links between each part of the economy are specified, with different time lags and adjustment processes. This can then be used to simulate how the economy would respond to different policy changes.

10.2 Supply-side stabilisation measures

Earlier in this chapter we suggested in a graphical way how a successful policy of supply-side adjustment would enable the economy to increase the supply of real goods and services at a given level of aggregate demand. To put it simply, a situation of excess demand can be removed by a rightward shift in the supply curve. There are two broad categories of policy which can expand the supply side of the economy. First, policies can aim to improve the efficiency of the existing resources and productive capacity.

Second, policy can be directed towards expanding the economy's productive capacity.

Measures to improve efficiency of existing resources use will, if successful, allow the existing productive infrastructure to increase its output. What, then, are the constraints on supply which need to be removed by supply-side policies? Viewed from an orthodox point of view, the problem lies in various types of distortion and imperfection which prevent the market mechanism operating effectively. Many of these distortions are the result of government policy – price controls, taxes, subsidies, trade restrictions – which distort the market price signals and lead to an inefficient and supply-restraining allocation of resources. Supply-side policies should be directed, therefore, at the removal of market distortions, enabling market mechanisms to operate more efficiently. Viewed from a structuralist point of view, the causes of supply 'bottlenecks' are said to be more fundamental and can often be the result of underlying social, political or institutional factors (recall the discussion in Chapter 9 of the causes of supply bottlenecks which contribute to inflationary pressures). It follows that the design of supply-side policies which will be successful in augmenting the supply capability of the existing productive structure involves more than the correction of 'distorted' price signals. Indeed, since many of the market distortions are inherent in the economy's structure, their removal may require greater, rather than less, government intervention to increase the potential supply response of the economy.

Policies to increase the productive capacity and longer-term growth rate of the economy concentrate on stimulating a higher level of investment. If investment is constrained by the availability of savings, policy needs to be directed towards increasing the level of savings in the economy. An increase in public sector savings would involve a fiscal surplus, a situation which exists in few developing countries. Policy to increase the level of private savings has concentrated on the removal of distortions in the domestic interest rate level.

The neo-classical analysis of savings behaviour and of interest rate determination differs from the Keynesian analysis given in Chapter 2. In the neo-classical model, private savings are a function of the rate of interest, and the rate of interest is determined by the

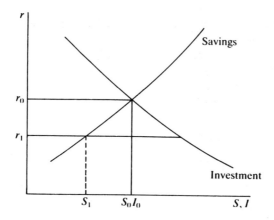

Figure 10.9   Savings and investment related to the rate of interest

demand for and supply of 'loanable funds', i.e. investment and savings. This is shown in Figure 10.9.

The equilibrium real rate of interest is r_0, which equates savings and investment S_0I_0. In many developing countries the real rate of interest is below the equilibrium level. This may be due to inflation rising faster than the increase in the nominal interest rate, or it may be due to a deliberate government policy to control the interest rate to a ceiling level. Suppose the rate of interest is r_1. At this rate there is excess demand for investment loans, and the available supply of saving (S_1) will have to be allocated by a system of rationing. However, if the interest rate is 'liberalised' and allowed to rise to r_0, both savings and investment will increase to the equilibrium levels S_0I_0. The removal of the policy-induced distortion in the market for financial savings increases the level of private investment and therefore leads to an expansion in the economy's productive capacity and output.

Structuralists are sceptical about the likely success of interest rate liberalisation policy, arguing that the effect of these measures may be damaging to the longer-term growth of the economy. If interest rates are raised in the formal monetary market, funds will be moved out of the informal sector. The level of savings in the formal sector will increase, but the total level of voluntary savings will be unchanged. At the same time, the effect of higher interest rates on working capital costs will impact adversely on supply. If the domestic financial market has an oligopolistic or monopolistic structure, the removal of controls on interest rate levels will allow the interest rate to be set at a level well above the market equilibrium rate, thereby discouraging investment.

Our simplified explanation of the contribution of demand and supply-side policies to achieving the stabilisation objectives implied that the policy maker could choose any combination of the two sets of policies. In reality, there are major constraints on the choice between demand restraint and supply augmentation approaches to stabilisation. First, the effects of supply-side policies are likely to appear only after some considerable time period. In the meantime, corrective demand management policies will need to be applied to restore macro stability to the economy. Second, there may be a conflict between the objective of achieving immediate stabilisation and that of increasing the long-term growth capacity of the economy. This can arise, for example, where an increase in investment involves an increase in imports of capital goods and essential inputs, while stabilisation policy is aiming to achieve an improvement in the trade balance by lowering the level of imports. A more obvious example of this trade-off is the decline in real output that typically accompanies short-run demand restraint policies, which adversely affects the growth performance of the economy.

Further reading

The 'industrialised country' model used in this chapter is similar to the analytical approach of the IMF to stabilisation policy. A good description of this approach is given in IMF (1987). For a discussion of the 'developing country' model see Taylor (1988). A slightly different account is given in Porter and Ranney (1982). The debate between the IMF and its critics also concerns the interpretation of the empirical evidence on the impact of stabilisation programmes in LDCs. Crockett (1981) provides a generally positive interpretation of the evidence; Taylor (1988) contains a number of case studies which question the effectiveness of the stabilisation programmes. The timing and sequencing of stabilisation policy is discussed in

Edwards (1986). The relationship between short-run stabilisation and longer-run growth is examined in Corbo, Goldstein and Khan (1987). An important issue not considered in this text is the impact of stabilisation policy on income distribution and poverty. This topic is discussed in Demery and Addison (1987) and Cornia, Jolly and Stewart (1987).

Notes

1. In the original version of the monetary approach to the balance of payments, Y was assumed to be fixed at the full capacity output level, and the price level was fixed by the international price level (all goods were assumed to be tradables). (This version is often referred to as the Polak model.)
2. The effect of changes in the price level on the position of the *IS* curve is not shown in the diagrams in this chapter (see Figure 5.11).
3. In the industrialised country model, individuals attempt to get more money when the supply of money is reduced relative to the demand for it, by either selling assets (bonds) or reducing expenditure. In the absence of a well-developed capital market, in developing countries individuals turn to the informal sector.
4. Refer to Chapter 7 for a discussion of the budget constraint. In this section a reduction in government expenditure occurs through a change in bonds so that only the *IS* curve and not the *LM* curve shifts with the initial change.

References

Artis, M. (1984) *Macroeconomics*, Clarendon Press.

Bautista, R., Hughes, H., Lim, D., Morawetz, D. and Thoumi, F. (1981) *Capital Utilisation in Manufacturing*, Oxford University Press.

Bird, G. (1983) 'Should developing countries use currency depreciation as a tool of balance of payments adjustment?', *Journal of Development Studies*, July.

Blejer, M. and Khan, M. (1984) 'Private investment in developing countries', *Finance and Development*, vol. 21, June.

Bronfenbrenner, M. (1979) *Macroeconomic Alternatives*, AHM Publishing Corporation.

Cho, Yoon-Je and Khatkhate, D. (1989) 'Lessons of financial liberalisation in Asia', *World Bank Discussion Papers*, no. 50.

Cline, W. (ed.) (1981) *World Inflation and the Developing Countries*, The Brookings Institution.

Cobham, D. (1987) *Macroeconomic Analysis: An Intermediate Text*, Longman.

Corbo, V., Goldstein, M. and Khan, M. (eds.) (1987) *Growth-Oriented Adjustment Programmes*, IMF and World Bank.

Corden, W. (1984) 'Booming sector and Dutch Disease economics: a survey', *Oxford Economic Papers*, no. 36, November.

Cornia, A., Jolly, R. and Stewart, F. (eds.) (1987) *Adjustment with a Human Face*, Oxford University Press.

Crockett, A. (1981) 'Stabilisation policies in developing countries: some policy considerations', *IMF Staff Papers*, March.

Cuddington, J. (1986) 'Capital flight: estimates, issues and explanations', *Princeton Studies in International Finance*, no. 58, Princeton University Press.

Demery, L. and Addison, T. (1987) 'Stabilisation, adjustment and the poor', *World Development*, vol. 15, no. 12, December.

Dooley, M. and Mathieson, D. (1987) 'Financial liberalisation and stability in developing countries', *IMF Working Papers*, March.

Dornbusch, R. (1982) 'Stabilisation policies in developing countries: what have we learned?', *World Development*, vol. 10, no. 9, September.

Dornbusch, R. and Helmers, F. (eds.) (1988) *The Open Economy: Tools for Policy-makers in Developing Countries*, Oxford University Press.

Edwards, S. (1986) 'Are devaluations contractionary?', *Review of Economics and Statistics*, vol. 68, no. 3, August.

Edwards, S. (1988) 'Exchange rate misalignment in developing countries', *World Bank Occasional Papers*, no. 2/new series, World Bank/The Johns Hopkins University Press.

Fry, M. (1988) *Money Interest and Banking in Economic Development*, The Johns Hopkins University Press.

Goode, R. (1984) *Government Finance in Developing Countries*, The Brookings Institution.

Grossman, H. and Barro, R. (1976) *Money, Employment and Inflation*, Cambridge University Press.

Houthakker, H. (1961) 'An international comparison of personal savings', *Bulletin of the International Statistical Institute*, vol. 38.

Houthakker, H. (1965) 'On some determinants of savings in developed and underdeveloped countries' in E. A. G. Robinson (ed.), *Problems in Economic Development*, Macmillan.

IMF (1987) 'Theoretical aspects of the design of Fund-supported adjustment programs', *IMF Occasional Papers*, no. 55.

IMF (1989) *World Economic Outlook*, International Monetary Fund.

Johnson, H. (1976) 'Elasticity, absorption, Keynesian multiplier, Keynesian policy and monetary approaches to devaluation theory: a simple geometric exposition', *American Economic Review*, June.

Khan, M. (1974) 'Import and export demand in developing countries', *IMF Staff Papers*, November.

Khan, M. (1987) 'Macroeconomic adjustment in developing countries: a policy perspective', *World Bank Research Observer*, vol. 2, no. 1, January.

Khan, M. and Knight, M. (1982) 'Some theoretical and empirical issues relating to economic stabilisation in developing countries', *World Development*, vol. 10, no. 9, September.

Killick, T. (1981) *Policy Economics*, Heinemann.

Kirkpatrick, C. and Nixson, F. (1987) 'Inflation and stabilisation policy in LDCs' in N. Gemmell (ed.), *Surveys in Development Economics*, Basil Blackwell.

Lahini, A. (1989) 'Dynamics of Asian savings: the role of growth and age structure', *IMF Staff Papers*, March.

Leff, N. and Sato, K. (1980) 'Macroeconomic adjustment in developing countries: instability, short-run growth, and external dependency', *Review of Economics and Statistics*, May.

Levacic, R. (1987) *Economic Policy Making: Its Theory and Practice*, Wheatsheaf.

McDiarmid, O. (1977) *Unskilled Labour for Development*, World Bank/The Johns Hopkins University Press.

McKinnon, R. (1973) *Money and Capital in Economic Development*, The Brookings Institution.

Mikesell, R. and Zinser, J. (1973) 'The nature of the savings function in developing countries: a survey of the empirical literature', *Journal of Economic Literature*, vol. 11, March.

Morley, R. (1988) *The Macroeconomics of Open Economies*, Edward Elgar.

Mundell, R. (1962) 'The appropriate use of monetary and fiscal policy under fixed exchange rates', *IMF Staff Papers*, vol. 9, March.

National Westminster Bank (1985) *The British Banking System*, National Westminster Bank.

Parkin, M. and Bade, R. (1982) *Modern Macroeconomics*, Philip Allan.

Perlman, M. (1974) *Macroeconomics*, Weidenfeld and Nicolson.

Polak, J. (1989) *Financial Policies and Development*, Development Centre Studies, OECD.

Porter, R. and Ranney, S. (1982) 'An eclectic model of recent LDC macroeconomic policy analysis', *World Development*, vol. 10, no. 9, September.

Renshaw, G. (ed.) (1989) *Market Liberalisation, Equity and Development*, International Labour Office.

Roemer, M. (1986) 'Simple analytics of segmented markets: what case for liberalisation?', *World Development*, vol. 14, no. 3, March.

Shaw, E. (1973) *Financial Deepening in Economic Development*, Oxford University Press.

Smith, W. (1966) 'A graphical exposition of the complete Keynesian system' in M. Mueller (ed.), *Readings in Macroeconomics*, Holt, Rinehart and Winston.

Squire, L. (1981) *Employment Policy in Developing Countries: A Survey of Issues and Evidence*, Oxford University Press for the World Bank.

Stevenson, A., Muscatelli, V. and Gregory, M. (1988) *Macroeconomic Theory and Stabilisation Policy*, Philip Allan/Barnes and Noble.

Taylor, J. (1979) 'Staggered wage setting in a macro model', *The American Economic Review Papers and Proceedings*, May.

Taylor, L. (1983) *Structuralist Macroeconomics*, Basic Books.

Taylor, L. (1988) *Varieties of Stabilisation Experience: Towards Sensible Macroeconomics in the Third World*, Oxford University Press.

Tun Wai, V. and Wong, W. (1982) 'Determinants of private investment in developing countries', *Journal of Development Studies*, vol. 19, October.

Williamson, J. (1968) 'Personal savings in developing nations: an inter-temporal cross-section from Asia', *Economic Record*, June.

Williamson, J. (1983) *The Open Economy and the World Economy*, Basic Books.

World Development (1982) 'National and international aspects of financial policies in LDCs', *World Development*, special issue, vol. 10, no. 9, September.

Index